Our world desperately needs Christians to live the abundant life Jesus promises. This book is vulnerable and practical about how each of us can move from exhaustion to peace. I recommend it to any leader or friend.

ANDY COOK, executive director of the Wheaton College Billy Graham Center

Ignite Your Soul is not an amalgamation of cheery theory and pithiness—this is real life. Caliguire vulnerably opens up the life she has lived and introduces us to the soul care practices that sustain her. (The Soul Care Reflections at the close of each chapter are wisdom worth the price of the book alone!) Soul care is a life lesson we cannot afford to skip.

CAROLYN CARNEY, national director of spiritual formation at InterVarsity Christian Fellowship and author of *The Power of Group Prayer*

Many of us may be unknowingly just one small spark away from devastation due to soul neglect. But as Mindy Caliguire reminds us, this is not the way of Jesus. With stories and Scripture, Mindy shows how any leader can become healthier to the point of thriving and lead others to greater Kingdom impact and fruitfulness.

MICHAEL MARTIN, president and CEO of ECFA (Evangelical Council for Financial Accountability)

People are weary. Wildfires rip through our lives. Weaving together personal story, biblical insight, spiritual practices, and insightful opportunities for reflection, this book points to a Trinity-focused way to healing, peace, and purpose.

ELLEN DUFFIELD, coordinator for the Centre for Leadership Studies at Briercrest Seminary, fc
of *A Theology of Thriving*

Ignite Your Soul is an essential exploration into one of life's most profound questions: *What is the state of your soul?* With wisdom and warmth, Mindy guides readers through the transformative process of learning to live from a healthy soul. I highly recommend setting aside time to read, contemplate, and absorb the profound insights here. It's more than a book; it's a journey to the center of your life.

BRENT McHUGH, CEO of Christar International

Mindy Caliguire is the kind of coach you want with you if you find yourself heading down the road of burnout. Her personal experience of restoration and passion for guiding others are contagious. *Ignite Your Soul* will surely inspire you on your journey to experiencing the flourishing life that Jesus offers.

DOUG SAUDER, lead pastor of Calvary Chapel Fort Lauderdale

Few things matter more than the health of our souls. Weaving together honest reflections and the wisdom of Scripture, Mindy Caliguire makes accessible life-giving practices that can open us to the deep peace of God even amid the hardest of times.

TREVOR HUDSON, author of *Seeking God* and *In Search of God's Will*

Mindy Caliguire not only helps us understand our soul but also invites us into a life saturated with attentiveness and responsiveness to the realities of God. If adversity, heartbreak, or anxiety have left you feeling tinder dry, this book is like a quenching salve. Step into Kingdom living where you can truly say, "It is well with my soul."

JOHN CARROLL, executive director of Dallas Willard Ministries

Ignite Your Soul resonates deeply with my own soul, reminding me that its healing and care is crucial to my leadership. I love the invitation to reflection, connection, and interaction. It is the way of life that God invites us into that leads to "life, more and better life than [we] ever dreamed of" (John 10:10, MSG).

MARGARET FITZWATER, executive director of
Train – Develop – Care for The Navigators US Leadership Team

Mindy practices what she teaches and teaches well what she practices. *Ignite Your Soul* is a much needed, and welcome, respite for those of us who wish to thrive on our journey of following Jesus.

GREG NETTLE, president of Stadia Church Planting

Mindy's knowledge of the fast-paced, high-churn world of leadership along with her passion for the redeemed souls of leaders come together in this indispensable resource for recovering the soul of your leadership. This book is well worth your attention, contemplation, and action.

CASEY TYGRETT, pastor, spiritual director, and author of *The Practice of Remembering* and *The Gift of Restlessness*

Mindy generously shares personal stories, hard-earned wisdom, and guided practices to illuminate the path to a flourishing life. Her authentic and vulnerable words help us learn the unforced rhythms of grace and bring to the world the peace of a healthy soul.

SAM SONG, mission pastor at Saddleback Church Central and founder of *The Beautiful Future* podcast

Reflecting on her own past reliance on self and relentless striving, Mindy offers valuable lessons and guidance on reconnecting with God and finding renewed hope. *Ignite Your Soul* demonstrates that embracing surrender and leaning on God will kindle the depths of our souls as we journey forward.

OLUSOLA OSINOIKI, chief responsibility officer at Josh Leadership Academy

Mindy's wisdom takes us forward into a deeper walk with God to deepen our souls. So grateful for her candor, clarity, and way to see Jesus in the busy world around me.

ANDREW CLARK, founder of The Lion's Den, Wherewithal.co, and Jeremiah Fund

Mindy Caliguire's personal desolation left her no further choice but to accept the long-standing invitation from God to replenish her soul. But as Mindy points out in this compelling book, accepting this gift is not a quick or easy one-time surrender. Mindy shows how age-old Christian practices of delight, silence, and rest, among others, can slow-walk us through the never-ending quest toward spiritual health.

MARGARET DIDDAMS, PHD, editor of *Christian Scholar's Review*

Mindy doesn't just talk the talk; she's walked the walk. She beautifully shares how despite (and through!) burnout, grief, and devastation, she's established helpful rhythms toward improved soul health. Every leader, whether in business or ministry, would be wise to follow her lead.

KEVIN ORRIS, chief advancement officer at Awana and coauthor of *Field Guide for SPACE*

I'm a leader who has tried to do the work of Jesus in a way that about killed Jesus' work *in* me. I know what it's like to put out a spiritual feast for others but sometimes feel anorexic myself. This book points a clear path to hope beyond despair, light beyond darkness, and life beyond death. Mindy is like a spiritual director, a gut-level-honest counselor, and a true friend who wants to see my soul thrive, and somehow she has managed to pack all that into these pages. If you sense that the game isn't only about what you're *doing* but who you're *becoming*, Mindy has found a path forward and graciously shares it.

BEN CACHIARAS, lead pastor of Mountain Christian Church

Many of us put forth efforts and practices to be healthy physically, but what do we do for our souls to be healthy? This book is for you whether you are a leader experiencing burnout or a follower of Christ looking to take better care of your soul. It is thought-provoking and offers practical tools to start practicing caring for your soul.

DEBORAH ROSS, minister ("Momma Strings") and author of *Back on the Streets*

IGNITE

When Exhaustion, Isolation, and Burnout

YOUR

Light a Path to Flourishing

SOUL

Mindy Caliguire
with Shawn Smucker

A NavPress resource published in alliance
with Tyndale House Publishers

NavPress.com

To first responders—those who tend to the body and those who tend to the soul.

In the 2021 Marshall Fire, Captain Jamie Wood and his teams saw a sudden shift in the wind at 2:30 a.m. and held the line in our neighborhood, preventing further devastation. They had been stopped five previous times because the wind and heat were so severe. But then the wind changed. And they were ready.

The first responders in my life have been many: mentors, friends, guides on a path to healing and restoration I so desperately needed.

First responders move toward—and even run into—messes and danger with the intent to rescue, heal, and protect. They are fearless, gentle, and good. May we all grow in our capacity and willingness to courageously do the same.

Contents

Foreword

I recently found myself in a pensive mood. I had experienced significant loss in my life as I'd watched several leaders, people I admired, fail from foolish decisions. And now, once again, I was experiencing the loss of someone I had admired: my grandfather. This loss wasn't the result of some kind of moral failure but simply due to age—he wore out.

Loss has a way of making us slow down and ponder.

We may find ourselves reflecting on what it is that we *actually* lost and why it's so painful. Maybe loss reminds us of our own vulnerability and our own vulnerability to loss.

But despite the pain that results, I believe loss can provoke us to deeper places.

My pensive mood led me to pick up a book, one that had been given to me about my late grandfather's leadership style and the various principles that were important to his success. It was in this book that I was introduced to the term *soul care*, along with the work of Mindy and Jeff Caliguire.

The term and the work appealed to me because it had become increasingly apparent that my soul had been affected by both losses and gains. I was introduced to the notion that my soul was not something to be ignored but something to be nurtured.

This resonated deeply with me, but a question remained.

How?

How could I nurture my soul?

This book, *Ignite Your Soul*, provides an answer.

I love how Mindy weaves the natural and the supernatural, gently guiding us on a meaningful adventure that twists and turns from the valley to the hilltop. Mindy lives it, practices it, and shares it. I believe that you will experience your own journey as the pages before you meld into a pathway that nurtures your soul.

Stephan N. Tchividjian
CEO and cofounder of the National Christian Foundation
of South Florida

Prelude

Fire is powerful and strange, showing up in our lives in two very different ways.

As a force of nature, fire devastates forests and communities. Open flames damage our skin, sometimes irreparably. The hottest temperatures leave very little behind. Fire is a weapon of war, a means of great destruction.

And yet we quite literally depend daily on the mechanics of fire to cook our food, keep our houses and hospitals warm, and generate the photosynthesis that keeps the entire human population on this earth alive and breathing.

Fire is a source of death.

And fire is a means of life.

When it comes to our souls, the fires of life can lead us to the same diverging paths. We find ourselves beyond burnout, have been exhausted longer than we can remember, feel desperately alone. The fire within can make us feel like we have nothing left, like anything alive within us has been consumed.

Or we can notice the fire and choose to attend to the burning within. The flames become lanterns. The charred ground becomes soil for new life.

In 2021 in Boulder, Colorado, where I live, hundreds of homes and countless acres were destroyed by wildfire. Nearly thirty years ago, my life unexpectedly imploded: a wildfire of the soul. Both of these tell the same story, and it is our collective story: Destructive forces can paradoxically illuminate a path for our lives to be set ablaze by the goodness, kindness, and nearness of a living and loving God.

Perhaps you find yourself among the charred remains of your life. Or perhaps you simply sense a dryness, a vulnerability, where one stray spark set to the tinder of your emotional, relational, spiritual self could set off the whole thing.

I am beyond certain of this: Our living and loving God can paradoxically light a path for you as he has done for me.

Whatever destruction you or those you love have faced—and despite whatever burnout, flameout, or dropout has resulted—you can step onto this pathway to healing and flourishing.

On the other side of death is life.

No matter the current state of your soul, may you, too, find your path toward healing and flourishing ignited.

Your soul matters.

Fan the flame.

A BURNED-OUT SOUL

Choosing Life

> [I was forced] to enter the basement of my
> soul and look directly at what was hidden
> there, to choose, in the face of it all,
> not death but life.
> **HENRI NOUWEN,** *The Inner Voice of Love*

December 30, 2021, was supposed to be a normal, quiet day
between Christmas and New Year's. My husband, Jeff, and I spent
the Christmas holiday relaxing around our house near Boulder,
Colorado, with nearby family and friends. As I anticipated the
coming year, I especially enjoyed imagining what it might hold
for my emerging organization, Soul Care.

That morning, I was leading an hour-long online retreat from our
house. Jeff was out running some errands. Normally those retreats,
even online experiences like the one I led that day, are rich times of
communing with God, opportunities to deliberately step out of normal life with a group of other people to ask that important question:
What is the state of your soul?

As I glanced out the windows near my desk in the basement of the house, I could see the sky growing darker and turning a strange shade of orange. Rattling windows and patio cushions flying from the neighbor's deck into our backyard confirmed that high winds had begun to blow. I wondered what kind of storm might be coming in. It was eerie.

But I was in the middle of debriefing the retreat experience with leaders who had called in from all over the world. It was tearful, tender, and filled with the tension: Could things really be better for me? Trying to focus, I had silenced all notifications on my devices.

I didn't know Jeff was urgently trying to reach me, calling my phone over and over again. A wildfire had gotten out of control a few miles west of our home, and it was racing east through the mesas in the high desert outside Boulder toward the suburbs. Firefighting efforts could not keep up with the blaze.

The fire had started that morning, most likely the product of someone burning their trash. As the fire dashed east through the dry brush, it flew through Whisper Ranch, our budding retreat on nearly thirty acres of undeveloped land in the Rocky Mountain Foothills, incinerating our beloved Dream Shed.

My retreat didn't end until noon. I had no idea any of this was going on.

Jeff kept trying to reach me. When he couldn't, he hopped into his truck and headed for our house.

There are conditions that make an area ripe for a wildfire, and those conditions were all present in Boulder County when the Marshall Fire began. Our previous summer had been warm with unusually high rainfall that had produced a large bloom of grasses. But we live at high altitude with very low humidity, and that thick ground cover of dried-out brush and grass became like the kindling you would use to start a fire. Minimal snow had fallen that winter, so very little moisture remained in or on the ground when wild winds began sweeping through our communities at 115 miles per hour, stirring up dust, drying everything out even more.

All that was required was a spark.

WHAT IS THE STATE OF YOUR SOUL?

What is the thing that matters most to you in your life, that feels like it sets the tone for your overall well-being?

Is it your relationships? Family members? Finances? Maybe when you think of what matters most, you think of your vocation, your job, your employment.

Whatever your answer, there's a profound reality far beneath those surface conditions: What actually determines whether you flourish (or not) in any area of life . . . is your *soul health*.

You may never have even considered that your soul could be healthy or unhealthy. Most of us don't give much thought to the state of our souls. Admittedly, soul health is hard to describe, hard to discern. But I've learned that quietly, powerfully, your soul's well-being is driving everything that matters to you.

The evidence around and within us, though, shows us just how easily overlooked that reality is. Many people's souls, like the dry underbrush of the landscape surrounding Boulder, are one spark away from devastation.

This book is an invitation to consider honestly the well-being of your soul, embrace with compassion whatever you find there, and see your burnout and exhaustion as an invitation to meet with God, experience rest, and explore a new path forward.

And we must begin with an essential question: *What is the state of your soul?*

If you envision your soul as a landscape stretching out in every direction, a wilderness untouched by humanity or modern conveniences, what do you see? Perhaps your soul feels precisely as it was created to be: a vibrant place of vitality and natural beauty, with mountains and rivers, wildflowers and grassland. While it's true that the soul is a mystery, we sense the terrain. We know, somehow, that the very core of us was created to teem with life and complexity—rolling hills and towering trees, birds singing from every branch, animals of every species thundering across the green plains. All is well. All is whole.

When you look at the ecosystem of your soul, do you feel joyful and whole? This thriving soul is in touch with God, connects authentically with others, and engages in meaningful work. There is a capacity for quiet, stillness, and inner peace, no matter the situations life brings.

Maybe that doesn't sound like your soul at all. Maybe you've become more cynical, noticed that you're more abrasive, feel like you're spiraling down further and further, continually isolating yourself from others. A person with a parched soul goes from burnout to burnout, gradually collapsing emotionally, spiritually, and physically. So perhaps the landscape of your soul is withered by drought; the ground is cracked, the vegetation dry and struggling to grow. All wildlife has fled. The ecosystem teeters on collapse. Dust clouds approach from far off, drowning out the sunlight.

Do these conditions sound familiar? When burnout and exhaustion begin to define our interior lives, we often use the same terminology to describe how we feel.

"How are you doing?" we might ask a friend. "How are you really doing?"

"I'm just so . . . dry," they reply. "I feel . . . parched."

"Running on empty."

"Living on fumes."

"No more gas in the tank."

We know what that means and how it feels. Most of us have been there at some point in our lives. But what many of us don't realize is that we're actually talking about the state of our souls. When we feel that severe lack, the kind of burnout we can't find our way out of, we often remain unaware that it's our souls that are cracked and undernourished, arid and hot and prickly. We're uncomfortable. Everything is unsatisfying.

Three thousand years ago, a Hebrew poet wrote these words in the ancient text of the Psalms that we identify as the desperation of a thirsty soul still today:

Why, my soul, are you downcast?
Why so disturbed within me?
PSALM 43:5

We know that a lush, thriving interior life is possible. We sense that our existence should be more connected, more aligned. We thirst for something more, something nourishing that hasn't materialized— and we're left wondering where our lives are headed. Shouldn't we feel more alive than this? Where is the full life we long for?

When the soul is severely parched, the former lush under- growth becomes tinder that can easily become engulfed in flames and cause terrifying destruction.

All that is required is a spark.

The year was 1995, and I had no idea I was on the verge of falling apart.

I was tired. I had been working hard, under financial pressure, and there was no end in sight. My husband and I had started a brand-new church in Boston, Massachusetts, which was a hard thing to do in a relatively hard place. We had launched this brand-new venture in the hardest possible way: completely on our own. Midway through our years there, I was running all the organization's back-end responsibilities—bookkeeping and communications—while also recruiting volunteers, training small group leaders, engaging our donors, and leading at least three small groups. We had a two-year-old, and I was six months pregnant with our second son. Some nights I'd stay up until 1:30 a.m. out at Kinko's writing and printing our newsletter to raise support, then I'd go to work first thing in the morning to write personal notes, address envelopes, and mail them out. I'd sprint through the tasks of another full day . . . and another . . . and another.

Meanwhile, like many church founders, Jeff was trying to lead from a very diminished place. My strong husband—a football-playing Ivy League graduate—couldn't get out of bed in the morning. He had become angry, even paranoid at times. Though we had no language to communicate what was happening, it's likely he was in a full-on chemical depression. All I knew was that he was struggling and I needed to step up in order to help keep all our many plates spinning.

Emotionally, I only felt comfortable in the "happy zone." Can you relate? I could allow myself to experience joy and hope and positivity but had no idea how to move into emotional territory marked by sadness, confusion, grief, or despair. Whenever someone asked how I was doing, I of course told them I was busy, but the truth was that my life was overfull and I was barely hanging on. Jeff was fighting his own battle with despair—there was no way I could afford to go there too.

So I fought harder. Ignored my anger, sadness, and any sign of exhaustion. Worked harder. Told myself it was only for a season. Tried harder. I helped Jeff plan meetings and write sermons, and I started yet another small group because . . . well, who else was going to do it? I was the pastor's wife and the unpaid volunteer who didn't have a title, running the entire "back office" of our tiny, fledgling family and church. I did what had to be done.

Until I couldn't.

And the tinder caught fire somewhere near my cerebellum and optic nerve.

When I woke up on Saturday, March 18, 1995, everything in my field of vision was moving. The images were clear but constantly, erratically shifting. I blinked hard, but the world kept on spinning. I closed my eyes for a minute and shook my head. What was happening?

When I opened my eyes again, nothing had changed. Across the hall, our son was crying for me to get him out of his crib, so I stumbled toward the door to get him—but instead turned into the bathroom and threw up. *What could be more normal than a pregnant woman throwing up? Surely this was nothing out of the ordinary.*

But by Sunday morning, it became clear that something was very wrong. I couldn't walk straight, couldn't see straight, couldn't stop throwing up. Still, Jeff had to leave to go get the church ready—the show must go on, right? Even in our church of maybe sixteen people, we couldn't pause for a Sunday. We couldn't say, "We need help."

I stayed behind, but a few hours later, I called a friend and asked if she could take me to the hospital. My doctors were urging me to go to the ER because I was becoming severely dehydrated and showing signs of premature labor. This was no longer just unpleasant; it was getting dangerous.

I vomited all the way to the hospital, all the way through the admission process, all the way up the elevator, and all the way to my room. My poor friend.

After the doctors halted the premature labor and rehydrated me with an IV, I returned home. But my symptoms did not improve. Neighbors, friends, my mother, and my mother-in-law all took turns coming to help us with meals and keeping the house running while I lay, completely useless, in bed. Three weeks into what would turn into months, my eyes began involuntary movements to try to keep up with my new, dizzying world.

I couldn't get out of bed. I couldn't walk from one room to the next. I couldn't watch TV or read or do anything. I could only eat if I was blindfolded; it was the only way for me to avoid getting sick from the constant motion.

I felt like a prisoner in my own body.

What I didn't realize was that my physical symptoms were shouting a deeper truth.

My body was speaking.

My soul, brittle and tinder dry, was on fire.

But that was not the end. Over the next few years, that fire ended up lighting a path that has marked my life ever since.

IS IT WELL WITH MY SOUL?

As I've worked these last many years with individuals and organizations all over the world, I have come to discover that my personal experience with overwork and the accompanying symptoms of severe soul depletion are far from unique. In fact, sometimes the more devoted someone is to serving others, the more likely they are to be operating out of a severe deficit rather than overflow.

How is it that almost everywhere I go, the people connected to God are dying inside? They are dry, parched, withering even—but the show must go on, the work must get done.

Here's what I've discovered: We are not thinking about the soul correctly. We assume that the soul is well, as the beloved hymn confirms, because we are saved. But if that's the case, why do so many of us feel like something within us is dying?

It's because there's a difference between a soul being *saved* and a soul being *well*.

For people like me who grew up in church, the only time we talk about the human soul is with reference to its eternal destiny. Souls are either lost or found, saved or unsaved, and in most contexts, once we've begun a relationship with Jesus, the "soul conversation" is over. Nothing more to talk about. The deal's been done. Our souls are set.

As a result, we have no imagination for the well-being of the soul, no rationale for the care of the soul, no language for what the symptoms of a soul that's unwell might be. And because of that, millions of devoted followers of Jesus are suffering on the inside. Terribly. While suffering is a part of the human condition this side of eternity, the inner devastation doesn't have to be. We can learn to keep our souls well tended in the midst of any and all circumstances.

How do we know this? Consider what Jesus had to say about the soul:

> "What good will it be for someone to gain the whole world, yet forfeit their soul? Or what can anyone give in exchange for their soul?"
>
> **MATTHEW 16:26**

Now, the answer to this famous rhetorical question is obvious: *Nothing.* No one benefits from gaining the world if they forfeit their soul!

But to whom is this question directed?

Often we think that Jesus is asking this of the person who doesn't yet know him. When we read it as an evangelistic appeal, we hear something like this: "How could you benefit by chasing after fame and fortune and missing eternity with God?"

But what if we're wrong? What if he's talking to those of us who already know him?

At the beginning of the paragraph in Matthew 16, we learn something important. Jesus is not asking this question to the big crowd, the curious and the doubters. No, he's talking to his disciples, people who are already in a deep relationship with him. He is literally talking to those who have left everything to follow him.

So what does Jesus really mean when he talks about them losing their souls? How could a disciple of Jesus—then or now—lose their soul?

The original Greek word translated "soul" in verse 26—*psychē*—helps broaden our view. Many Bibles include a footnote on verse 26 clarifying that the word translated as "soul" is *psychē*. And, importantly, it is the same word used in verse 25—except there, *psychē* is translated as "life":

> "Whoever wants to save their life will lose it, but whoever loses their life for me will find it."

We readily associate verse 25 with hard-core discipleship: the life of sacrifice and true devotion. So why do we so often consider the same word in the following verse an evangelistic appeal? Radically changing audiences from one sentence to the next doesn't make any sense.

What's going on here? *Psychē* is translated interchangeably as both "soul" and "life" because the biblical concept of the human soul is inextricably woven together with the concept of one's overall "life."

Your soul, your *psychē*, your life, is everything that makes you you. We find the same concept in the Old Testament with the word *nephesh*.[1]

The ancient, biblical concept of the soul is consistent in the Old Testament and the New: The soul represents one's whole person, one's whole life, the entirety of one's existence. It's not an amorphous thing that floats away when we die or that gets flipped on by an inert toggle switch when we first surrender our lives to God. The soul invisibly integrates and holds together all the dimensions of our personhood.

Your soul is not simply an inner state of being with a binary status. Saved or unsaved. Lost or found. Heaven-bound or not. My friend the philosopher and scholar Dallas Willard describes the soul with a beautiful metaphor in *Renovation of the Heart*:

Our soul is like an inner stream of water, which gives strength, direction, and harmony to every other element of our life. When that stream is as it should be, we are constantly refreshed and exuberant in all we do, because our soul itself is then profusely rooted in the vastness of God and his kingdom, including nature; and all else within us is enlivened and directed by that stream.[2]

Far too many people who are devoted to God, who have resolute beliefs about God, who have even been saved by God, are experiencing anything but that lush interior world. They don't just have souls that are parched—their souls feel like they're burning to the ground.

The flames continued to spread east, spurred on by hurricane-force winds. Dear friends who lived adjacent to Whisper Ranch called 911 to report smoke coming up the hillside. When the operator found out where they lived, she begged them to leave. Immediately. They left with their dog, a cell phone, a guitar, and—they quickly realized—their lives. They circled back at a safe distance to watch in horror as their home, located at the magnificent crest of the mesa, was engulfed in flames.

Meanwhile, Jeff finally reached me by phone. Could these friends of ours evacuate to our house in the next town over? Of course, I said! But by the time they arrived, we were considering evacuation as well. The soot floating through the air and the color of the sky were unnerving. According to reports, a nearby Starbucks was surrounded by fire. The wind kept blowing harder and harder.

Not long after Jeff and I decided it would be best to head out, the evacuation notice came.

What would you grab if you had to leave your home for a fire? is a great question to ask as an icebreaker, but real life definitely did not get my best thinking. In a panic, I grabbed four pairs of boots . . . and eleven pairs of underwear. That was it. You can imagine the well-deserved jokes I get about that now. Where did I think I was going? (One friend did sympathize, noting I took the essentials and the most expensive things. She was being generous, but I'll take it.)

My mind was in fight-or-flight mode, not a good space to make practical decisions. But often it's the place we find ourselves when life hits that level of chaos and unpredictability. When everything threatens to come burning down around us, uselessly grabbing underwear and boots can sometimes be the extent of our ability to reason and plan.

Our car joined some thirty thousand individuals on the road that afternoon who had also evacuated homes, fleeing the approaching inferno. It took us ninety minutes to drive four miles. Friends in Lafayette who were on vacation in the mountains graciously offered their empty home to us. We accepted. After briefly getting our bearings there, settling in, and checking in on loved ones throughout Boulder County, we learned that Lafayette was now under evacuation orders too. It was time to go again, and we decided to trek up into the mountains to join our friends there.

As Jeff and I hit the road once again, the scene was almost unbelievable. The entire area flickered orange against the coming darkness, as if an underground volcano had seeped up through the fields and the streets. High flames reached up into the evening sky. We passed through Denver at a safe distance, but the fire back in Boulder County appeared to have destroyed much of what we left behind.

Soon we realized there was yet another obstacle on this newest road to safety. We would be driving at night through the hairpin turns and steep cliffs up to Berthoud Pass at an elevation of eleven thousand feet on dark, icy roads amid hurricane-level winds that would further threaten the stability of our pickup truck. As we stopped to reevaluate our plan, we were emotionally and physically exhausted, uncertain of where else we could even go—or how long we would need to be there.

Only when I reached out to a friend in Denver did we finally find a place to rest.

"We've been watching the news, thinking of you guys," she said without hesitation. "Come. Now. You'll have the top floor for as long as you need."

When we finally ended up back down in Denver, washed out from a day of chaos and anxiety, we turned on the news, desperate to find out where the fire was going and how our community was coping. As we sat on our friend's sofa, completely exhausted, the images on the TV confirmed our worst fears.

Our neighborhood was burning.

LIVING PARCHED

We're discouraged when we hear the news of people we love and respect suddenly failing, their lives going up in flames. *How could they do that?* we wonder. Did they have a momentary lapse in judgment? Make a one-off mistake? How could someone give up so much for what seems like so little?

The reality is that, for many, the landscape of their life was primed for disaster. Perhaps under ordinary circumstances, a small flame wouldn't have caused such destruction. Maybe they encountered something they could have said no to, or walked away from, or told the truth about. But when a person's soul is in a state of unhealth and dis-ease, a lot of dead things start building up; it can be enough kindling to fuel an incredible amount of destruction.

Maybe you recognize the feeling.

The death of a dream.

The feeling that God has abandoned you.

Failure.

The loneliness of leadership.

Feeling trapped in a career path.

Burnout at work.

A sense that your faith is faltering.

Strains on relationships.

Anxiety over the future.

Even success can create piles of tinder in a soul.

It's taken me a long time to be comfortable exploring the connection between the Marshall Fire and the state of the human soul. Now, having lived through this past year—the initial fires, the terrible aftermath, and the slow work of rebuilding—I see the parallels quite clearly: The pre-burn conditions common to the land before a wildfire can also be found in our souls. We, too, are at great risk when traumatic circumstances catch us in a drought of the soul.

A dry soul creates a thirst we cannot seem to quench. Only when we care for our souls do we find ourselves in proximity to life-giving water.

An ancient Hebrew poet observed what a life immersed in God is like:

> *That person is like a tree planted by streams of water,*
>   which yields its fruit in season
> and whose leaf does not wither—
>   whatever they do prospers.
>
> **PSALM 1:3** (EMPHASIS ADDED)

"Like a tree planted by streams of water . . ."

Without water, we wither. Our souls become dry. Arid. Hot. Prickly. Uncomfortable. Bordering on lifeless. Ultimately unproductive or even counterproductive.

Sometimes, in the early stages of drought, we are able to keep putting out the spot fires in our souls. One little disaster averted here, another one avoided over there. These flares pop up, and we're just barely able to keep things under control. We keep telling ourselves it will all be fine, everything is fine.

Some of us can put out spot fires until something unforeseeable—a global pandemic, a job loss, a sudden death of someone we love—disrupts all our rhythms.

When a high wind sweeps into our lives, even a small spark can cause everything to go up in flames.

No one intends for a wildfire to ravage their soul. It's not fun. Thankfully, the destruction that tore through my parched soul was not the end of my story. Nor does it have to be the end of yours.

SOUL CARE REFLECTIONS

1. In your life so far, what has most shaped your understanding of the human soul?

2. Consider what things in your life may be creating conditions for a wildfire of the soul. Write them down and identify a trusted friend or counselor with whom you can talk about these things.

3. What would your life look like if you were "planted by streams of water"? What tangible steps could you take to become more like that tree?

4. Is it easy or hard for you to imagine the well-being of your soul driving everything that matters to you? Do you agree or disagree with this idea?

5. What are symptoms that indicate your soul hasn't been all that well? What are markers of health and vitality?

6. If your body could talk right now, what would it be saying to you? How loud would it have to get in order for you to listen?

2

RECOVER YOUR LIFE

Learning Unforced Rhythms of Grace

Fundamental aspects of life, such as art,
sleep, sex, ritual, family ("roots"), parenting,
community, health, and meaningful work are
all in fact soul functions, and they fail and fall
apart to the degree that soul diminishes.

DALLAS WILLARD, *Renovation of the Heart*

After four hospitalizations over the first few months of 1995, with no meaningful improvement to my physical symptoms, I reached the utter depths of desolation.

God, what is going on? I thought we were on the same team! I have been working hard to serve well, but stuff is not getting accomplished right now. This is not strategic.

Neurologists who had been called in to consult with my doctors could not explain my bizarre set of symptoms, so they could offer no hope for if, how, or when I might improve. I began to spiral emotionally.

How does this end? What will happen when this baby comes?

"Sounds like you feel like you're in a desert," observed a friend as we spoke on the phone.

"Totally! So . . . how do I get out of the desert?" I asked, desperate for just the right advice.

I could hear her kindness through the phone.

"Mindy, if God takes you to the desert, go to the desert and learn what the desert has to teach you."

Those were not the words I wanted to hear.

When we are in great pain and suffering, it's hard to believe there's any way that God could meet us there. But the desert became the place of reconnection that my soul so desperately needed. In the dryness of a desert, I found fresh hope.

I sensed God nudging me toward a verse I'd asked the small groups I was leading to memorize:

> "I am the vine; you are the branches. If you remain in me
> and I in you, you will bear much fruit; *apart from me you
> can do nothing.*"
> JOHN 15:5 (EMPHASIS ADDED)

In the quiet of that moment, the Spirit gently whispered, *What part of "nothing" didn't you understand?*

As it turned out, there was a lot about nothing that I didn't understand.

I was reassured by Scripture that there was nowhere I could go from God's presence (see Psalm 139) and that there was nothing that could separate me from him (see Romans 8:35-39). If I was never actually apart from God, why was "doing nothing" on the table?

But whether I understood it or not, there was no denying my current reality: I was doing a whole lot of nothing.

And out of that nothing emerged a willingness to ask new questions, seek new kinds of help, and ultimately find a new way of life. A way of life that would keep me connected to God in real time—not just to ideas or thoughts about God, however sincere.

And that's when I began to recover my life.

Those neurologists had urged me to seek emotional support since, no matter what the actual cause of this vertigo was, my declining mental state would definitely impair my odds for recovery. At that time, finding a Christian counselor anywhere in New England seemed unlikely, but it just so happened that Dr. Lombardi's office was within walking distance from where we lived. We had no money for me to receive counseling. And even if we had, I ordinarily wouldn't have taken time away for something just to help me. But this was different, and the risks were high. Once I had enough stability to walk, I visited his office, desperate for help.

I remember holding on to the exterior wall for support as I tentatively moved down the stairs toward his tiny, one-room basement office. My strength and stability had been ravaged by months of imbalance and inactivity. He probed into my family of origin and asked about the last five years since coming to start this church. He shared his sympathy about the physical symptoms I was experiencing—and for the first time since this began, I heard something that felt like the beginning of an answer.

"Mindy," he said in a tender but authoritative voice, "I can't speak from a biological perspective when it comes to your symptoms, but from a psychological perspective, you have forced out of your body what would never come out of your mouth."

I was confused.

He continued: "The word *no*."

I could feel the tears welling up in my eyes. I nodded, but I didn't say anything.

"Your body is saying no," he continued. "Your body is saying, 'I can't keep doing this. I can't keep holding it all together.'"

These days, we're understanding so much more about how the body holds trauma, how the body "speaks," and how the body has a wisdom that has been long ignored. But even in that season in my life, before that kind of language or understanding was widespread, I began to experience the reality of those things. As I continued to grow and heal, I noticed the Bible's references to the body in new ways.

For example, I was well aware of the verse that promises, "Trust in the LORD with all your heart and lean not on your own understanding; in all your ways submit to him, and he will make your paths straight" (Proverbs 3:5-6). But now I noticed the following two verses in a new way, since they speak of the health of the body: "Do not be wise in your own eyes; fear the LORD and shun evil. This will bring health to your body and nourishment to your bones" (Proverbs 3:7-8).

Health to my body? Nourishment to my bones? I was learning that by remaining mindful of God, I could experience something different, even in my physical body.

Another verse, Galatians 2:20, became an anthem for me as I recovered my life: "I have been crucified with Christ and I no longer live, but Christ lives in me. The life I now live in the body, I live by faith in the Son of God, who loved me and gave himself for me."

I didn't know if I would get my life in the body back, but I was resolved that if I did, I would live by faith. Real-time, in-the-moment confidence in and connection to God's very real presence.

HE MAKES ME LIE DOWN

When we are extended beyond our physical, mental, and emotional limitations—I think God, the gentle and good Shepherd, will in fact *make* us lie down if we don't have the sense to do it ourselves:

> The LORD is my shepherd, I lack nothing.
> *He makes me lie down in green pastures,*
> he leads me beside quiet waters,
> *he refreshes my soul.*
> He guides me along the right paths
> for his name's sake.
> Even though I walk
> through the darkest valley,
> I will fear no evil,
> for you are with me;
> your rod and your staff,
> they comfort me.
>
> You prepare a table before me
> in the presence of my enemies.
> You anoint my head with oil;
> my cup overflows.
> Surely your goodness and love will follow me
> all the days of my life,
> and I will dwell in the house of the LORD
> forever.
>
> **PSALM 23:1-6 (EMPHASIS ADDED)**

Making someone rest when rest is a desperate need can be an expression of love.

Hear me on this: I'm not suggesting that all human illness or ailment stems from soul unhealth. But I am saying that our interior worlds and our physical world are far more integrated than we often realize, more than our ways of thinking about God and the world typically afford.

If we can learn to listen to our bodies, our emotions, and our mental health, we'll begin to learn more about the current state of our souls—and discover a new path forward.

RECOVER YOUR LIFE

As I began to reflect more on my life, I realized I had been operating from my own wisdom, my own strength. One author has described this as "functional atheism,"[1] a term that definitely described me. Sure, I was committed to serving God and the people around me, and if anyone asked, I would have said I believe in, trust in, and rely on God.

But, in direct opposition to those sentiments, I worked harder, strived more, tried to do as much as I could, and leaned on my own strength and wit and abilities. I know I'm not alone in this. When we're living this way, eventually most of us end up at the same place: exhausted and at the end of ourselves, maybe a bit resentful that in the midst of our faithful service we are completely tanked.

I have good news for you: There are other options.

I'd like you to take a moment and read this passage from *The Message* translation that has, for some time now, offered me a compelling vision of the kind of life I want to live in this world, working together with God to bring about good. I suspect you want to live a similar life? If so, let yourself hear the invitation in these words from Jesus:

"Are you tired?

Worn out?

Burned out on religion?

Come to me.

Get away with me and you'll *recover your life*.

I'll show you how to take a real rest.

Walk with me and work with me—watch how I do it.

Learn the unforced rhythms of grace.

I won't lay anything heavy or ill-fitting on you.

Keep company with me and you'll learn to live freely and lightly."

MATTHEW 11:28-30, MSG (EMPHASIS ADDED)

How many of us, after years of striving and controlling and sometimes even manipulating, can identify with that first verse? Tired. Worn out. Burned out. Notice the antidotes to these conditions:

- *Come to me.*
- *Get away with me.*
- *Take a real rest.*
- *Walk with me.*
- *Work with me.*
- *Keep company with me.*

None of these are demands. They are all highly relational invitations.

And the potential?

- *Learn the unforced rhythms of grace.*
- *Carry nothing heavy or out of place.*
- *Live freely and lightly.*

Friends, this kind of life is entirely possible, no matter how dry the undergrowth, no matter how isolated you feel, no matter how hard the fire is blazing, no matter how still and silent the ashes of your former life lie around you. You may have a bit of a journey ahead of you to get there. But setting your heart and mind, your self and your soul in this direction is absolutely available to you.

Read these words again:

> "Are you tired? Worn out? Burned out on religion? Come to me. Get away with me and you'll *recover your life.* I'll show you how to take a real rest. Walk with me and work with me—watch how I do it. Learn the unforced rhythms of grace. I won't lay anything heavy or ill-fitting on you. Keep company with me and you'll learn to live freely and lightly."
> MATTHEW 11:28-30, MSG (EMPHASIS ADDED)

Can you hear Jesus' invitation to you?

No matter where you are or how you feel as you read these words, know this: There is hope.

When we realize there's very little we can do in our own power, even to tend to the pain and burnout in our own souls, we find our eyes increasingly open to the many ways in which God may restore our lives.

That's what I discovered. When my eyes started moving involuntarily, I needed to have an MRI to rule out a rare form of adolescent brain cancer—for which this kind of eye movement, called opsoclonus, is often both a symptom and a diagnosis. Doctors didn't usually see it in adults my age. Even after our son was born, I had another MRI with a "tracer" (unsafe during pregnancy), to further confirm, thankfully, that no tumors were present.

What was causing my eyes to move? Well, it's actually a pretty common phenomenon called *compensation*, where the brain will accommodate the physical body to "compensate" for something the body is experiencing. Basically, my eyes were moving wildly in response to my brain trying to adjust to what the optic nerve "thought" it saw—which was everything moving. So eventually my eye muscles began to behave in a way that would have followed that "motion." Bizarre, right?

There are other situations in which the brain compensates for what it thinks is real. One of those is when people experience depression. Some people can be genetically predisposed to depression, and they need medicinal help in order to rebalance their brain chemistry. There's no shame in this, just like there's no shame in wearing glasses or taking insulin if you have type 1 diabetes or are insulin dependent. But for many, what starts as circumstantial depression—a series of hard things, a depletion of reserves in a particularly demanding season, a lack of support—can become true chemical depression . . . in as little as three weeks. In other words, the brain will begin to biochemically reinforce that depressed state. It will compensate for, or accommodate to, what has become a "new normal." Involuntarily, a set of hard circumstances can become embedded in our biology.

Over the years, I have learned that this is common knowledge in the medical profession. For our purposes, it's a big deal, because once you enter into a chemical depression, it should be addressed. Sometimes getting outside more, exercising, improving sleep, and doing other practical things can help lift us out, but not always. Sometimes we need medical intervention, and that is entirely appropriate. (Acknowledging we need help, no matter the form it takes, can be a turning point.)

Gradually we make the transition from operating in our own power, from striving and fighting and closing our fists, to accepting God's invitation to rest and planting ourselves by his healing streams (Psalm 1:3), where, moment by moment, day by day, we are able to function in light of the reality that God is indeed real.

REPLANTING ON BURNED GROUND

At our friend's home in Denver, we remained glued to the television, watching the flames tear through the communities north of the city. Around 11:30 p.m., nearly twelve hours after the initial blaze began, Jeff and I sat up straighter and leaned toward our friend's TV. One of the reporters was live and on-site in our actual neighborhood.

When we saw a neighbor's distinctive RV in the background of the shot, we realized it was possible our home was still intact. The next morning, we could confirm: Our house remained standing. It was one house away from being completely destroyed, and while it had sustained serious smoke damage, it had survived.

Not everyone was so fortunate. Sixty-two homes in our small neighborhood had been reduced to ash. Six thousand acres of land had burned. Nearly 1,100 buildings had been destroyed, including our only structure on Whisper Ranch.

The next day, New Year's Eve, a light snowfall and the work of dozens of firefighters and first responders brought an end to the fire. But it had taken its toll, and our community faced years and years of rebuilding and recovery.

Restoring land after that kind of destruction is long, expensive, and difficult. Some things, usually the most personal, can never be recovered—physical photos, heirlooms, gifts from children. The loss can be devastating.

And, of course, the same is true of our souls. What is most precious to us in a flourishing life can be lost in the fires of burnout: relationships, a vocation, peace of mind. A soul that is dry is on the edge of destruction, and soul destruction can lead to years and years of loss, heartache, and reconstruction.

But we are not destined for destruction or the loss it brings. The flames don't have to claim us so quickly. When we learn how to connect to life outside ourselves, we find our souls well hydrated and the ground ready for restored life, which means we can prevent some forms of destruction while also enduring the hard circumstances that come our way.

No one sets out to trash the well-being of their own soul. But it happens through honest, even hardworking and faith-believing, neglect. Soul health, on the other hand, involves purposeful, intentional ways of living connected to the source of life. It's the tree planted by a stream.

Where can we start in order to prepare our souls for the days ahead? And if we have already experienced destruction, what can we do in order to see the landscape of our souls return to life and vitality?

Naturally, we want to quickly move to more comfortable places. We want to know the way out of the desert.

But often the first step is to enter the Garden of Desolation.

SOUL CARE REFLECTIONS

1. What have you been thirsty for lately? Recognition? Relief from pain? Maybe a renewed connection to God?

2. What makes you most alive to the real-time presence of God? A walk in nature? Wild animals? A sunset? A beloved friend or family member? Beautiful music or dancing or writing or painting? How could you incorporate more of that in your life today?

3. Which do you relate to more: the psalmist's depiction of the tree planted by living water (Psalm 1:3) or a deer panting for water (Psalm 42:1)? Why? Where in your life do you notice your vitality? Dryness?

4. If you are parched, how long have you felt that way?

5. Read through Psalm 23 slowly. Circle or highlight any word that especially stands out to you today, and pause for a moment to talk with God about why it is significant.

6. Tinder for a soul wildfire can take many forms: disappointment, shame, sadness, regret, bitterness,

a feeling of being trapped, or even broken relationships. Are any of these things in your life? Do you recognize any ways they are priming you for destruction?

7. To assess the current state of your soul, visit soulcare.com /assessment-nav.

3

THE GARDEN OF DESOLATION
Making Space for Grief

Sometimes we have to allow grief to have
its way with us for a while. We need to get
lost in the landscape of grief. It is a wild and
rugged wilderness terrain to be sure, but
it is here that we meet our truest selves.
And we are met by God.

AMANDA HELD OPELT, *A Hole in the World*

In the earliest days and weeks after the Marshall Fire, recovery efforts occupied our lives. We searched our smoked-out home and tried to make temporary living arrangements. We divided our things between what we needed day to day, what would go in storage, and what needed to go straight into the dumpster. We spoke with insurance companies and made lists and itemized our lives.

And we also began exploring Whisper Ranch, assessing the damage, trying to figure out what to do next. Our plans for that beautiful place had involved creating some sort of a retreat, a place where people could come to explore and experience soul revitalization.

But as I walked the property after the fire, it felt as though that

33

dream was dying. Much of the life-restoring beauty had gone up in flames: grasses scorched, our one structure completely destroyed, so many trees burned seemingly beyond any ability to recover.

Honestly, I was in shock. It was devastating to walk among those charred trees. A deep grief threatened to overwhelm me, not only because of the trees but also because of everything that their destruction represented: our scorched hopes for the property, our friends who had lost so much, and our suffering community. Those trees would remain a continual reminder of the fire that had swept through our lives.

I had no desire to wallow in my grief or dwell on the tragedy. Our community was in mourning! Our property had been destroyed, and the home we had been living in was seriously damaged! *Start again* seemed the most appropriate words. We needed to clean up the mess the fire had left us and begin again.

I'm an energetic, glass-half-full person, and my natural personality quickly leapt to the forefront: It was time to think positively, make a plan, and initiate forward movement to solve the problem. We had to keep going, figure out what our next steps would be, create a goal, and then delineate the best path from here to there.

I was ready to clear the land and start from scratch.

However, the truth was that I didn't know what to do or where to begin. I kept walking that high desert landscape, weaving in and out of the burned groves of trees, passing by the destroyed shed, soaking in the devastation.

We called in our friend Trevor, who was helping us with property management at the time, and he recommended that we go through and, using yellow spray paint, label the trees that needed to be cut down. Anything beyond restoration would be removed.

Trevor made his way along the hillside, his paint can making that clickety-clack sound as he shook it, the smell of spray paint rising. He marked every tree and some whole hillsides that were charred beyond the hope of regeneration and should be removed. There were easily several hundred in all. Each yellow mark on a black trunk brought a wave of sadness over me. It felt like pouring salt over an open wound.

After he had finished, Jeff and I met up at the top of the hill and looked out over the property. All those yellow marks were jarring. So many trees marked for death. Seeing the scale of what we were about to do caused something to shift in me, and a realization bubbled to the surface.

"What if we just waited to remove all these trees?" I asked, and the two of them looked at me in surprise. Trevor had just spent hours on step one of the plan to move forward, a plan I had wholeheartedly supported. And now I was questioning it.

Trevor shrugged. "There's no rush, and there's really nothing else we can do this time of year anyway."

"What do you think?" I asked, turning to Jeff.

"We can wait," he said, shrugging.

"Let's press pause," I said quietly, and a sense of relief filled me, though I couldn't have told you why or even what I was hoping for. "At least these tall, blackened reminders of loss can provide a habitat for wildlife."

Over the coming months, as I continued walking the property, working the footpaths up and down on rocks and grasses, staring at the distant mountains, I let the peacefulness of that place, even in its devastation, wash over me. It spoke to me of loss—and hope.

These hills would endure. These places held history. Land is not in a frenetic rush to get "better."

I sensed something in me begin to heal.

ERASING GRIEF

When devastation sweeps through our personal lives, how often is our first impulse to move on, run away, pretend everything is fine? Something irrevocably awful happens, and we desperately want to remove all traces of that pain. We want to forgive and forget (or maybe just forget). Clear it out and move on to the next thing. Somehow, we think that complete erasure of disappointment or pain or failure will make it seem as though the cause of those emotions had never even happened.

We somehow believe that erasing how we feel will lead to peace.

Our faith contexts all too often reinforce this impulse. For the most part, Western Christian systems emphasize and encourage (perhaps demand?) that we move quickly through grief. We don't have a high tolerance or appreciation for the weight of sadness, the ache of loss, or the anguish of lament. Somehow we've internalized a belief that if we can't simply smile or pray our way out of difficult times, something must be wrong with us, our theology, or our faith.

Even when we use David's laments in the Psalms as an example of leaving room for raw honesty with God, we are often quick to emphasize his recovery from the grief. We skip ahead to any place where the psalmist writes, "And yet will I praise him." We don't want to linger in the pain. We would rather believe that we will never hit rock bottom, that we will never have regrets, that we will never wrong anyone else or be wronged in a way that leads to serious hurt.

But we ignore the reality of devastation to the detriment of our souls' health. We live in a world where babies die, where wars displace hundreds of thousands of people, where diseases mercilessly eat their way through the lungs and spines of friends and colleagues. When we remove our metaphorical burned trees, we tear everything from the soil of our souls. The illusion of peace only lasts until the next storm comes along and begins to erode anything that is left. Soon—months or even years later—the pain comes racing back in some different form. So many of our addictions and poor decisions come from a place of not wanting to feel the pain in our lives; instead of letting ourselves feel the heaviness, we eat or shop or watch TV or keep working long into the night. Because we never take the time to sit with our grief, our down-the-road lives pay the price.

Grief ignored is a dangerous thing.

Life will sometimes be sad, disappointing, even crushing. If we don't sit with our grief long enough, if all we do is bury it or try to clear it away, there are long-term ramifications for our souls. When we avoid our pain, we refuse our souls the needed space to process or metabolize what we are feeling. The wounds we carry fester under the surface and sneak out in irrational fears, avoidant behaviors, and the inability to provide loving and caring space for our children or other loved ones when they invariably encounter loss and pain.

If we gloss over truly horrific realities, we subtly reinforce the idea that God's presence is only available to us when everything is going well. What a colossal deception. The comfort of God is nearer than the air we breathe! When we refuse to give space for our pain, we can even become incapable of facing or unwilling to face hard truths, which is extremely dangerous for our decision-making abilities.

A refusal to enter grief ensures more pain and loss down the road.

One day, walking down past Jeff's newly built shed on our property, I found myself in the midst of a grove of those dead trees, an open area where there was a small clearing among the charred trees of nothing but flat sand and some surrounding boulders. If grass had ever grown there, I couldn't tell. Before the fire, it had been a dense grove of native ponderosa pine, too thick to walk through. Every single tree in that area had Trevor's yellow mark spray-painted on it, and yet as I stood there, a thought passed through my mind.

This feels like a sacred space.

How could that be possible? How could something sacred dwell in such ugliness and loss? My eyes welled up, because among the sadness and hopelessness of that utter devastation I felt a sense of aching holiness. I looked around at the blackened bark, looked up through the charred twigs into the bright blue sky, and I felt God there in that tiny grove, sitting with me in the middle of all those hard things.

Eventually, as something drew me again and again to stand among the charred trees, I gave the space a name: the Garden of Desolation.

Somehow this place was quietly reassuring to my soul. It was a space where natural qualities drew me to stillness, reflection, even acceptance. Where feelings of sadness and grief—even hopelessness—were welcomed, invited, and held by the aching beauty of the charred trees.

A short time later, we had some guests on the property who had never been there before, two executives who were interested in using the land to create spiritually significant times for their teams.

Even in that season after the fire, the rugged beauty of the land was undeniable. My hope was returning—hope that this could still be a place where souls would be revitalized.

Eventually we came back down to where the old shed had burned, and I led them into the blackened grove of trees. And I noticed a shift in myself. During the entire tour, my voice had been light and excited. I was so enthusiastic about the potential for this land to help people find soul healing, and I was eager for these two leaders to see it too. But as we walked into that isolated grove of trees with the sandy floor, my voice dropped to a hush.

I started riffing quietly about the desolation I sensed in that space, and how necessary those spaces of desolation are to the health of our souls.

"I call it our Garden of Desolation," I explained. "Sometimes there are parts of our lives that need to be grieved, but we can be so quick to make a plan or move on to the next happy thing. I think we need a place like this to invite us into lament and grief so that we don't just bury our feelings but really feel them and experience them. We've all had situations that felt like fires destroying everything in our lives, but so many times we just rush forward to level the trees and drag them away instead of sitting in the midst of the pain and grieving what's been lost."

We stood there quietly as a cold February wind rattled the branches together. White, puffy clouds raced across the sky above us. I looked over and realized with surprise that one of the men, the more senior of the two, had tears in his eyes.

"Are you okay?" I asked.

He nodded, hesitated, and then said, "I wasn't going to mention anything about it, but our daughter miscarried twins last week. They would have been our first grandkids. It happened while I was out of the country, and I am just so sad for her and for all of us. I hate seeing her in such pain."

He was weeping openly now, and we just quietly stood there with him in his pain. As I felt his sadness, I noticed two things happening: the remaining two of us thought about the pain in our own lives, and yet we were also, with our presence, giving him space and time to speak up about his grief.

Once he was able to speak, he said, "I haven't really thought about it, just sort of pushed it down whenever it came to the surface. But it's been really hard. And really sad. And you're right—I just keep moving on, staying busy so I don't have to think about it or face it."

As I took more people into the Garden of Desolation, I saw something happen again and again. Even if we were just doing a quick tour, I would give them the opportunity to pause and think about the heavy things they were carrying. Things that have been utterly destroyed, things that have no hope of return. Some people needed only a moment of silence; for others, the pause became transformative, a point in time they could look back on and say, *Yes, that's when I finally faced the sadness and loss and recovered something in my soul.*

Here's what I know:

Everyone is carrying something.

I'm carrying something.

You're carrying something.

Everyone is carrying something.

FACING GRIEF

Grief ignored is a dangerous thing—but something powerful, even transformative, can happen when we acknowledge our grief. We may even experience healing we couldn't have imagined in the moments when we were suffering the loss.

There is something sacred about entering our Gardens of Desolation. External devastation becomes a mirror for the soul, inviting us to acknowledge the grief we have tried to bury or ignore or move on from too quickly. Facing that grief honestly is an important part of the journey toward soul health.

Eventually, Trevor walked back through the property to scratch off most of the yellow paint from the trees. We decided that the devastation left behind by the fire would be an important reminder to us, even as the land rejuvenated itself and flourished once again.

We won't just remove the hard stuff.

The pathway to the other side of grief winds through it.

Over the years, there have been a few sources of wisdom that have invited me to encounter my own suffering, powerlessness, and grief, moving me away from my tendencies toward toxic positivity and into a more grounded place for my soul. One particularly significant influence came from friends who have gone through twelve-step programs.

Their courage and authenticity have shown me a different way to live when everything has fallen apart; what it is like to admit we are at rock bottom, that we have become powerless; what it looks like to take a fearless and searching inventory before telling ourselves, God, and someone else the exact nature of our wrongs.

It's right there in steps one, four, and five:

1. "We admitted we were powerless over alcohol—that our lives had become unmanageable."

4. We "made a searching and fearless moral inventory of ourselves."

5. We "admitted to God, to ourselves, and to another human being the exact nature of our wrongs."[1]

You can't do this in thirty seconds and move on. You simply can't complete these steps without truly experiencing the grief that led you into this space.

The alternative to entering the Garden of Desolation is denial, which is another key concept in twelve-step recovery. Denying our pain and our grief, denying that anyone has ever hurt us or that we have ever done anything to seriously hurt others. What lies beneath the denial is a deep fear that if I give myself over to how sad I am about certain parts of my life, I won't survive; I won't recover. The grief will swallow me.

But in fact, it's only when we are honest about our sadness and grief that we can find true hope and peace. The Garden of Desolation helps us move beyond a life of denial and into a life of acceptance, surrender, and peace.

Lewis Smedes, author of *Forgive and Forget* and *The Art of Forgiving*, is one of the teachers and authors who have helped transform my thinking in this space. He has taught me that we can be honest about our sadness and grief, be transparent about how we have hurt others and been hurt ourselves, and still live with hope and gratitude. He writes,

> Forgiving does not erase the bitter past. A healed memory is not a deleted memory. Instead, forgiving what we cannot forget creates a new way to remember. We change the memory of our past into a hope for our future.[2]

To move into hope, we must first forgive. To be able to forgive, we must acknowledge that something happened, something painful.

This is what the Garden of Desolation has taught me: Being willing to consider not only the positive but also the negative aspects of my life is a direct indicator of soul health. The greater my ability to enter into my grief and sadness, the healthier my soul becomes. If I am unable to consider desolation in my life when it happens and in the days, weeks, and months that follow, the health of my soul will suffer.

To face our pain, we do not need a literal Garden of Desolation. I find my soul drawn back to Lamentations 3:19-24 (MSG) when I need to reckon honestly with my grief:

I'll never forget the trouble, the utter lostness,
    the taste of ashes, the poison I've swallowed.
I remember it all—oh, how well I remember—
    the feeling of hitting the bottom.
But there's one other thing I remember,
    and remembering, I keep a grip on hope:

God's loyal love couldn't have run out,
    his merciful love couldn't have dried up.
They're created new every morning.
    How great your faithfulness!
I'm sticking with GOD (I say it over and over).
    He's all I've got left.

This is such a beautiful vision of what happens when we remember "the trouble, the utter lostness, the taste of ashes." Yes, those are hard things to dwell on, but in the ensuing moments we are reminded of God's loyal love, his mercies, and his faithfulness—not necessarily to remove the difficulty or immediately rescue us from it, but to be with us in it.

Moving through the Garden of Desolation is a slow process, and it's something we have to take our time with. Grief cannot be rushed.

We have to let ourselves truly experience the negative feelings. We have to let all the hard emotions in, put words around them, name them.

The Garden of Desolation can be a place of aching beauty, remembrance, and even healing. Summon the courage to go there.

A NEW THING

March arrived on the property, and then April. The snow on distant mountains began to disappear as temperatures rose. Spring was on the wind. Tiny green shoots of grass began poking up through the desert dust, the smallest cacti began to return, and wildflowers started appearing, so fragile and tender in such a harsh environment.

I kept my eyes on the trees. Would anything happen in the spring? Would these trees that looked completely dead show any signs of life? It was hard to imagine them surviving when two-thirds of a tree was burned or an entire grove was completely charred.

Then something strange began to happen. I noticed something silken and smooth forming on the tree trunks.

Sap was flowing. This sticky resin began leaking through the bark on the trunk of even the most charred trees, a trickle that looked like tears.

How could this be? I wondered. *How can a tree destroyed by fire still flow with sap in the spring?* The land somehow felt even weightier, more aching and honest—sap welling up off trees without any needles, burned in fiery winds.

And not much later, on some of those damaged trees, tiny little bright green needles began growing out of the tips of the barren, blackened branches. The contrast of the colors was almost eerie: fresh, pale green signs of life somehow emerging from brittle death.

Unbelievable. Even a few of the trees that had been hastily "marked for death" by the fearsome yellow spray paint had new growth. Far from being over, this story was just beginning.

We didn't know how many of the trees would survive. A few years later, we still don't know for sure. But these small signs of life spread throughout the property in those early months after the wildfire, declaring that even after devastation, a new thing can begin growing.

It reminded me of my life in the months and years after my body and mind had broken down in 1995, after all the hospitalizations, after our second son had been born.

Even after an experience that feels like death, life begins showing up again.

 ## SOUL CARE REFLECTIONS

1. Are you someone who tends to avoid grief and sadness, or do you enter it fully? Why do you think you respond the way you do?

2. Can you identify a desolation event in your life that you never fully grieved? Write about it.

3. Read Lamentations 3:19-24 a few times. What words stand out to you? Journal about their importance and what they have to say to you about grief.

4. Talk to someone about the moment of desolation that you've never properly grieved. Allow yourself to feel the sadness of that experience in the presence of a trusted friend or counselor.

5. How could you create space for a Garden of Desolation in your own life? What would that look like?

A PAGE, A PERSON, AND A PLAN

Practicing Attention

> Man cannot be happy for long unless he
> is in contact with the springs of spiritual
> life which are hidden in the depths of
> his own soul.
>
> **THOMAS MERTON**

During the year and a half after my initial collapse from benign vertigo, and as I engaged in counseling, I realized that I needed to retrain my brain to stop responding to the deeply ingrained force of drivenness inside me. I don't know how else to explain it. My brain was hardwired to accomplish, to strive, to seek out a goal, to problem solve, and then to fixate on that goal and dedicate my whole self to reaching it.

I'm not here to tell you that being goal oriented is an awful, terrible, no-good thing. It can be a wonderful trait and bring about a lot of good in the world! But I had reached a point where I would push toward my goal no matter the collateral damage. I sacrificed so much to accomplish the things I accomplished.

When drivenness is our primary way of being in the world, there will always be collateral damage. Our neglected and abused bodies and families will begin to fracture, our relationships will shrivel, our organizations will eventually flounder. Our souls will suffer.

This method of living had put a crack in the foundation of my life and eventually sent me straight to the hospital. All those years of striving had been like bending a living green stick farther and farther until it snapped. I hadn't broken completely in two, but I was severely damaged. I couldn't survive that way any longer. Nor did I want to. The allure of drivenness had been exposed as the fool's gold that it is.

In the year after my initial hospitalization, I still could not see straight (literally), and I was hospitalized several more times for dehydration caused by severe nausea. The neurologist warned my husband and me that we would need to prepare for the worst. Whether or not I recovered, this baby would be arriving soon. We had to begin making preparations assuming I might not be able to do even the bare minimum to care for a newborn.

Jonathan Robert Caliguire was born on the twenty-fifth of May; it was one of the most memorable and significant moments of my life. There were times during the pregnancy when I wondered if either one of us would survive, and the moment I held him, I knew at least he would be okay.

Like green needles emerging after the wildfire, Jonathan's birth was one of the early signs of life. Slowly, life was returning. But I was no longer the same. I had no idea what the future would hold, but if I did get my life back, I prayed that going through this experience would matter somehow. If I did regain my vision, my balance, and my focus, I knew deep in my soul that I would never return to the prior blurry, out-of-balance, frenetic version of my life.

After Jonathan was born, vertigo still came and went, and I

was weak from spending months in bed. Eventually, after three or four months, I was finally able to drive, and I could leave the house to go to the grocery store. That initial period was very slow, very much about healing, and very full of gratitude for the new path to life that was opening up before me. I found myself doing an inventory of who I was and what had been driving me so hard all those years. How had I ended up at rock bottom? What had made my life so conditioned for a wildfire to come along and destroy everything? Would these episodes be inevitable for the rest of my life, simply a result of some physiological state that was out of my control—or could I discover a different way of living?

THE WAY OF ATTENTION

It's all well and good to decide you no longer want to be a certain way. But changing the way we are, changing the way we interact with the world and those around us—that kind of change doesn't come easily. Making any kind of significant shift requires us to pay attention—both to what caused the devastation and to the inner voice of the Holy Spirit, who leads us to practices and ways of being that will open us up to change. I needed to value my own life enough to start really paying attention to what was happening in and around me. This was all part of learning how my soul mattered in the midst of all the other priorities in my life, which also mattered.

By the time fall arrived and we began drawing closer to Christmas, I realized the first thing I needed to do: take care of my physical body. Falling into physical disrepair happens so easily when we are consumed by what must get done. We don't set out to become physically unhealthy, to let our muscles atrophy, to abandon a balanced relationship with food. But it's easy for all these things to happen. When we are overwhelmed, we don't make time for the things our bodies need.

As I recovered and many of my prior responsibilities with our ministry had been picked up by others, I embarked on the first venture into caring for my soul, which was very physical: Even though we had no money (we were church planters, after all), I joined a local health club.

I still remember entering that gym for the first time, weak and uncertain. All I could do was walk on the treadmill, and sometimes even that felt like too much. My legs shook, and I clung to the supports on the sides of the exercise machine. All around me, spandexed human beings, pictures of health and strength, bounded from one station to the next. I could hear the sound of metal clanking and crashing to the floor around me as incredibly strong people finished repping weights I wouldn't be able to get off the ground.

But for the first time in my life, I didn't care about my weakness. I didn't feel self-conscious about what I could do in comparison to what others could. Instead, I was overwhelmed with gratitude that I could walk, incredibly grateful just because I *could*.

I felt like I'd had so many things taken from me during that year: my strength, my ability to care for my family, my ability to care for our home, my positions of responsibility (and control) within our fledgling church. Walking allowed me to finally do something simply for the joy of doing it. After dealing with body issues since I was a teenager, it felt so different to do this thing, to exercise, simply because I could and because it made me feel good. Not to lose weight. Not to become better or more successful at a sport. Not to fit an ideal.

I walked simply for the sake of walking, and I did it for myself. There was immense freedom in this. I wasn't taking care of someone else. I wasn't being more productive or efficient. I walked because I wanted to—and because I enjoyed it. Because I could once again.

It is nearly miraculous what simply moving our bodies can do. Did you know that walking can tame your sweet tooth, reduce the risk of developing breast cancer, ease joint pain, and boost immune function?[1] Sometimes I would enter the gym feeling down, discouraged, or overwhelmed by life's circumstances, but after walking for forty-five minutes, the world didn't seem so bleak a place. And I grew in confidence, too, because I could feel myself getting stronger.

A simpler life became my new normal. During my illness, I'd involuntarily let go of everything I *had* to do. Once I began to recover, I stayed in a very small space. Simply taking care of myself and our family, nothing more. I still attended one of my small groups, but I didn't lead anymore. Someone else took over the finances of the ministry and the communications at church. Slowly, I was settling into a completely new rhythm.

Meeting with a counselor had started me on the right path. Walking was just another part of the process. The wildfire had torn through, and I was now wandering around, looking for signs of life and marking things that needed to be removed.

ATTENDING TO THE SOUL

Many of us, in our own reconstruction after a difficult time, attend to the weaknesses in our minds and bodies . . . and then stop. It's easy to stop pursuing soul health when the major disruptions and pain points feel resolved. I almost did.

But a quiet Sunday several months after those first signs of healing brought me face-to-face with the scope of my soul problem.

Our son Jonathan was around nine months old. Both of our boys had a fever, so I had stayed home from church. Church leaders had scheduled a meeting after the service in order to make decisions, set goals, and create some leadership structures—a meeting I would have liked to be at because I knew that any strategic decisions would have a direct impact on our family. I was finally healthy enough to attend these kinds of things without getting too worn out. But the boys were sick, so I stayed home with them.

It was midmorning on that Sunday, and the sun was shining through the windows. I bundled the boys up in blankets, and we sat together on the couch with a Dr. Seuss book that I had read so many times before I could read it without really thinking about where I was or what I was doing.

The boys were cuddled up against me in that sort of drowsy, feverish state, listening to my voice dance through the clever rhyme scheme. They were pleased to be there with me, the three of us spending time together. It was one of those wonderful, lazy mornings. Or at least, it should have been. But there was one problem: My head was not in the room at all.

I was worried about Jeff and wondering how the meeting at church was going. What decisions were being made? What would the ramifications be for our family? *If I leave now, could I catch the end of the meeting? Who could watch the boys?*

My mouth might have been reading the words in the book, or at least reciting them, but my mind was in a room thirty miles away, worrying, wondering, and mulling over what was going on there.

Then, as if by some special grace, I realized what I was doing. I had a significant time with my sons, and yet I wasn't experiencing it—I was somewhere else. My body was present, but my heart and soul were absent. In essence, even after recovering from the setback of vertigo, I was still living a fractured life, unable to simply be in the here and now.

A question popped into my mind.

Mindy, how sick would your kids have to be before you would actually be present with them—before they could gain your sole and undivided attention? It continued, *Can you not just read them a book and enjoy their presence?*

I'm not sure this was God's Spirit talking to me, and I'm also not sure it wasn't. The tone was strong, if not slightly harsh, pressing toward conviction. In that moment I was faced with the truth: The problems that had led to my vertigo were significant, they were internal, and they had not gone away. A kind of vacuum remained in my life, an empty space created from my illness. If I wasn't careful, excessive work, striving, and busyness would race right back in to fill that space once again.

When the vertigo had first knocked me sideways, it had been easy to blame the church and all the pressure. But I realized there on the couch, reading Dr. Seuss, that while those pressures were absolutely real, this—my inability to stop thinking about the work—was an inside job. As I walked this path of physical, emotional, and ultimately spiritual recovery, I came to see that I had terrible boundaries. I was codependent. And I did not have an accurate view of priorities . . . even when they were snuggled right up next to me.

Those three things—recognizing that my brain needed to be rewired, walking on a regular basis for no other reason than that I could, and noticing that I was not living in the present—helped me realize how unhealthy I was on the inside. The more I thought about it, and the more I read about it, the more I began to understand something new.

My soul was not well.

During those subsequent early days of my recovery, I came to believe that of all the things I was responsible for, the first and foremost among them was actually the well-being of my soul. I, like many others in leadership, had subconsciously expected to give and serve and contribute and lead from a place of deep soul unhealth. As long as we believe in the right things and work hard toward the right goals, that's all that matters, right? I began to question—or, in fact, rebel against—that view so strongly that a new determination formed within me: I would attempt to have as healthy a soul as I possibly could, even if I had no idea how, and then I would simply trust the outcomes of my life to whatever unfolded. I would stop *driving* toward achievement and performance. I would begin caring for my soul and let the chips fall where they may.

For anyone facing the need to build a new way of life, this decision cannot be overlooked, or else they will quickly move to another set of things to do—and still miss the point.

The point of caring for your soul, of finding a path out of isolation and burnout, is to build a life of deep attentiveness and awareness and openness to the reality of God in and around us at all times.

In my case, it was a meandering path, to be sure. But in hindsight I now see that rewiring my brain, moving my physical body, and being present, really present, in my day-to-day life helped bring me to a base level of soul health. Over time I distilled the many ways to care for my soul into three essential elements. These would lay the foundation of my spiritual formation for years to come and become core to how I believe anyone can recover the life of their soul.

To build a life of attentiveness and responsiveness to God, you'll need a page, a person, and a plan.

A Page

The "page" represents the invitation to reflection, usually in the inviting blank pages of a journal. Keeping a journal will help you pay careful attention to your journey. It will slow your mind down to the speed of your handwriting, giving you space to ask yourself and God the deeper questions.

But honestly, who really keeps journals?

With all due respect to preteen girls with diaries about their crushes, journals offer far more depth and possibility than we often imagine. Some of the most diligent journal keepers have been explorers: Marco Polo, Lewis and Clark, the crew of the *Belgica* as it sailed farther into the Antarctic than any ship had ever gone before.[2] Scientists keep journals of their experiments and findings to track what they have learned along the way. The *New England Journal of Medicine* and other scientific journals publish significant research. We keep pregnancy journals, scrapbooks, photo albums (even the photo albums on our phones) as ways of marking the key moments in our lives.

But what role does all this remembering, all this recording of a journey, have to do with ongoing spiritual development?

Like explorers, we are entering uncharted territory: the future. And because our lives really do matter, because our observations and discoveries have value, we would be wise to record our experiences, ideas, and prayers.

Writing helps us examine the course of our lives—past, present, and future. Like explorers and scientists, we engage in the process of recording observations, reflecting on new understandings, and considering next steps as we face our own uncharted territory of the future.

Taking time to write reflectively in a journal can also help us see the truth of our own stories in a way we cannot while we're living them. Allison Fallon, in her book *The Power of Writing It Down*, says, "Writing helps us step outside of our stories and see them differently. It helps us reclaim our stories for ourselves again."[3]

Interestingly, as an article on Kaiser Permanente's website points out,

> the *Journal of Experimental Psychology* published research that shows how writing your thoughts down can reduce intrusive thoughts about negative events and improve working memory. Even the simple act of writing something down lets your brain know you want to remember it. That's why note-taking is such an effective practice when learning something new.[4]

I can't imagine what my life would be like if I didn't have this outlet. I don't know how people keep going if they don't take the time to write about their lives, their hurts, their victories, and their pain. It's so important that we say (or write), "This is hard. I don't know where to go. I'm afraid. This is bigger than me. My life feels like it's falling apart. I don't see any way forward." And also "I'm so grateful. This is such a blessing. I have renewed hope. I have fresh energy."

A journal can be the place where we, like the psalmist, pour out both gratitude and desolation. When we are facing grief, journaling gives us a daily outlet to address the pain in our lives and helps us avoid living in denial. If we don't voice our concerns, we can begin to believe the lies that we will be stuck in these places of desolation, these habits, these addictions, for the rest of our lives. And reflecting on the beautiful and good reminds us that blessings and hardship often coexist, and it's important to pay attention to both.

My early journaling efforts began in the form of prayers. I would simply write whatever it was that I wanted to say to God—a lot of requests, a lot of intercession for others, a lot of gratitude, and a lot of seeking. Nearly any kind of reflection or observation can be valuable! It's almost impossible to fail at journaling.

But in hindsight I've noticed what can be the biggest mistake in journaling: not being honest. And there are plenty of reasons we might not be honest in our personal writing! What if someone finds the journal and reads it? Or what if I write the truth and come face-to-face with thoughts or feelings I've been trying to hide, even from myself?

I distinctly recall starting to write about something I was afraid of. I was taking a brave step and facing something head-on, writing it all out in my journal. I got about halfway through what I wanted to write, stopped, and crossed it all out. Then I started writing Bible verses in the journal instead. *There is no fear in love. But perfect love drives out fear* (1 John 4:18). I was trying to negate the very real fear I was feeling, to cover it up with Band-Aid Bible verses.

Some psychologists call that a "spiritual bypass," which is

> the use of spiritual practices and beliefs to avoid dealing with our painful feelings, unresolved wounds, and developmental needs. It is much more common than we

might think and, in fact, is so pervasive as to go largely unnoticed, except in its more obvious extremes.

Part of the reason for this is that we tend not to have very much tolerance, both personally and collectively, for facing, entering, and working through our pain, strongly preferring pain-numbing "solutions," regardless of how much suffering such "remedies" may catalyze.[5]

I think God would have loved to have met me in my fear, to speak love to me in that circumstance, possibly to address the situation itself with guidance or perspective or reassurance. Instead, I talked myself out of it, pretended I wasn't feeling it, and shamed the part of me that felt afraid. But we cannot so easily bury fear. And our fears must be faced if they're going to be meaningfully met by God.

Journaling requires honesty—with God and with yourself. And honesty requires paying attention. Eventually, I learned to push into a more honest self-reflection. These days, journaling is still a practice I return to nearly daily (but without any judgment about frequency). Usually when I write, I'm sitting on my couch at home or in a chair in my hotel room or out in the Dream Shed at Whisper Ranch, praying and writing about what happened the day before, what concerns I have for the day or days ahead, and the requests I have for the people and issues I'm holding before God. Multiple cups of coffee are usually involved. The practice grounds me even when my surroundings are changing and helps me truly pay attention to my life and to where God is at work in and around me.

Occasionally, I'll return to what I've written in the past, curious to look back at something I dreamed about or an event that happened or revisit a time when I felt God's presence in a powerful way. Journaling keeps me from living a disembodied life where I'm going through the motions without thinking about how my actions and thoughts, my hopes and discouragements, are impacting my life and the lives of those around me.

Spiritual writer Janet Hagberg believes that a leader's capacity for influence is actually capped by their capacity for reflection.[6] If we do not develop our ability to pause, reflect, and consider the bigger picture of our choices, our behavior, and our lives, we lose out on a key dimension of authentic influence. Our leadership will reach a point where it can no longer grow.

A page is an invitation to reflection. In the practice of writing honestly before God, we find ourselves in an open, nonjudgmental place where true healing can take place.

A Person

One of the biggest surprises in my soul recovery came in the category of "a person." This kind of person is a safe third space—usually someone outside our home and work environments—someone with whom we can process the authentic stuff of life. With this person we form an intentional relationship that helps us pay attention to, and be responsive to, what God is doing in our lives. These relationships have the power to open us up to new levels of healing, of growth, of becoming.

These kinds of relationships are a significant part of how we enter a recovered life. Whether trusted counselors, spiritual directors, coaches, or friends, these people help us notice what's going on in our lives and discover God in the midst of it all. They get to know the good, the bad, and the ugly. They are with us on the journey, and they are fundamentally *for* us—both for who we are now and for who we are becoming.

Do you have a person like that in your life? If so, count yourself blessed, and hang on to that relationship! And if not, don't give up hope. For many years, this would not have been a priority for me at all.

For the first five or six years Jeff and I were married, we moved across the country every August. During that time, people would often say to me, "Oh, this must be so hard for you, all this moving! Uprooting over and over again!" And I remember thinking, *This isn't hard at all!* Several years and several moves into this journey— hearing this question again and again—I began to wonder: Is something wrong with me? Was it maybe just a bit too easy for me to pack up my bags with Jeff and move on? I always had fun where we were, and I made friends, but when it was time to go, I honestly felt very little loss.

Shortly before moving to Boston, I read *When Your World Makes No Sense* by Henry Cloud. Out of his years of clinical work, Cloud shares his observation about the four main areas we tend to get stuck in developmentally: bonding, setting boundaries, resolving good/bad, and becoming an adult.

The topic of bonding really got my attention. The author of the book makes a strong argument: If you can't bond with people you can see, how will you bond with a God you can't see? As I took an assessment related to the reading, I remember proudly answering the questions about bonding with what felt normal and right to me: an incredible amount of self-reliance and independence. But when I tallied my score, my results were decidedly in the "Do you have a pulse?" section.

That moment was like a bucket of cold water to my face. On

an overcast day, I looked out my office window at the parking lot below and let the reality really land in my mind and heart: My sense of what was good and right was actually upside down.

My spiritual growth will reach a ceiling based on my ability to connect with and even depend on others. And it felt entirely possible I was at my ceiling.

Many of the people I interact with today would say this as well. We tend to live very isolated, protected lives, even when we are surrounded by people who truly do love and care about us. Vulnerability is an inside job.

So when we arrived as new church planters in Boston, I determined to change this relational isolation and venture into more authentic relationships. If relationships were far more vital than I had previously given them credit for, then I wanted to move in that direction.

One morning, I saw a young couple walk into a church we were visiting. Something about the woman got my attention. *She looks like a lot of fun,* I thought. Her name was Lisa, and she unknowingly became the person I would learn how to build an authentic relationship with.

Through Lisa, over time, I learned how to pay attention to what was really going in my mind, in my heart, in my soul. She helped me see what I couldn't see, helped me understand the path from brokenness to healing in a new way. She was the friend who drove me to the hospital that first time, many years later.

Why is attending to our relationships—finding a person—so important for our soul health?

In their book *How People Grow*, Henry Cloud and John Townsend make the argument that relationships are the foundation of growth. Relationships, they say, are actually God's Plan A for how people grow, not the backup plan, or what we might think of as Plan B.

Growth is inherently relational. It does not happen on some mechanical predetermined path. Dr. Jim Wilder and Michel Hendricks write:

> When we do not create a spiritual family with strong attachments, we cut off the flow of transformational power.[7]

And the authors of *The Physical Nature of Christian Life: Neuroscience, Psychology, and the Church* note, "We are formed into mature, virtuous, and wise persons, not by some disembodied mystical process, but by life together in a body of persons."[8]

People help us grow. Heal. Become.

I wonder how many of us believe this?

In my own journey to recover my life, the power of ordinary relationships is what surprised me the most. So much of my own healing came about through interactions in ordinary, everyday relationships. I could tell I was *becoming* something new. Friendships, which I had so long ago dismissed as unimportant, became foundational.

In my book *Spiritual Friendship*, I talk about four of the reasons a person is so crucial. Here's a summary:

- *Mirroring.* We can't see ourselves. Friends help us see what we can't see about ourselves, and their feedback can help us become who we want and need to be. As you learn more about yourself, perhaps through therapy or coaching or spiritual direction, your friends can help you process these things.

- *Self-disclosure.* This is where soul friendship is born. It happens in the beginning, when we talk about who we are, what we love, and where we come from. Friendship then deepens as we talk about our families of origin and our experiences growing up. All this helps move us in the direction of the next step in friendship: confession.

- *Areas of struggle.* The ultimate form of self-disclosure is in confession. We all need to be known in our areas of greatest temptation, weakness, and failure. Our friends can stand with us at the edge of the cliff and remind us we don't want to go down there again.

- *Giving and receiving grace.* Whenever someone is willing to talk about their history and then move into confessing their temptations, weaknesses, and failures, we are on holy ground. If we can give grace in those moments, friendships move to a deeper level and can become a place where we go to receive the grace we need.[9]

I firmly believe we will not recover our lives until we have a safe place in which to process the actual circumstances and dilemmas we face. The safe place of a person—whether a friend, therapist, spiritual director, coach, or any other meaningful and authentic connection—is transformational and an essential ingredient to living from a healthy soul.

While a page is an invitation to *reflection*, a person is an invitation to *connection*. Both increase our capacity to truly attend to, or pay attention to, what matters most.

A Plan

I have a mixed relationship with planning, a reality that comes up frequently in my journaling and conversations with God, even now! I had to work hard to unlearn my dependence on planning. I had to get away from the intentionality that marked my drivenness and self-reliance. Sometimes, even still, creating a plan makes me a bit twitchy. The idea of planning—of mapping out where I want to go—can feel like a fearful return to those days when I was trying to squeeze every second out of the day, make the most of all my opportunities, and work relentlessly toward a goal. I do not want to return to that. That's a refusal deep in my soul.

In my break from hyperintentionality, I've been animated by the desire to learn and lean into things like reflection, surrender, trust, relinquishment, whimsy, the joy of hanging out, and spontaneity. Maybe I had to learn how to *not plan* before I could return to *making a plan*.

My "plans" now intend different and better things. But a plan is still important, I've learned.

Neuroscience teaches us that the brain organizes and galvanizes—often unconsciously—around the things we bring to the forefront of our minds as a goal or an intention. As we seek to care for our souls, we plan toward a preferred future—but this kind of plan expands well beyond what I used to write about in my Day-Timer years ago.

In recent years, many communities of faith have returned to an ancient approach to intentionality: the rule of life. The Latin *regula* refers to both a rule as well as a trellis. In farming or gardening, a trellis allows a plant that would otherwise languish along the ground to climb around a solid structure so it may optimally fruit or flower. How productive or fruitful would a grapevine be if it had no structure to guide its growth and production? What a mess a vineyard would be!

A rule can provide the same structural support—a rule of life supports our life and growth. Ancient communities began to "wrap" their corporate life with God around a set of practices that provided structure necessary for optimal growth. The oldest living "rule" dates back to the fourth century after the life of Jesus—before megachurches, before the Reformation, even before the Dark Ages.

A trellis is inert: not alive and not the cause of life. But the nature of certain living things is such that they will—by design—wrap themselves around those structures and "climb." And so do we. The human soul will languish on the ground or become haphazard and unfruitful unless it wraps itself around some firm structure—a set of practices that, in and of themselves, do not impart life but which do help the human soul thrive and produce life.

Any serious athlete, musician, or team similarly adheres to a rigorous structure of movement, nutrition, mental health, and many other things in order to achieve and maintain peak performance. And the same is true of the spiritual life. We can develop practices for our individual lives or discern them with our communities of faith. The practices we wrap our lives around do not in and of themselves impart life. Instead, they become solid structures around which we anchor ourselves and then reach for the next season of growth, remaining mindful and alert to the fundamental reality in which we as human beings truly operate: a whole life immersed (baptized) in the Trinitarian reality of God, living and flourishing within the Kingdom of God.

A trellis also provides the basis and guideline for pruning. I tend to have lots of wild tendrils running about, seeking their own day in the sun. But not all are what's best for me. Only the Master Gardener can wisely prune away the tendrils that begin to stray from the trellis, from the rule, from the intended growth.

In recent years, authors such as Steve Macchia, Adele Calhoun, John Mark Comer, and others have provided helpful instruction and insight on the *why* and *how* of designing a meaningful rule of life.[10] But really, whenever we make a deliberate commitment to live our lives in a certain way, with a certain outcome in mind, we are operating from the equivalent of a personal rule of life—whether or not it's written down.

I don't have a formalized personal rule of life, but my way of life involves the following:

- practicing silent prayer
- journaling regularly
- engaging with Scripture
- making space for spiritual friendships and community
- staying open to opportunities for hospitality
- vocational alignment—serving with my energies and gifts
- willing labor, including caring for our chickens
- maintaining a routine for my physical health
- getting enough good sleep
- monthly half-day retreats
- annual New Year's Day retreat

How about you? What things do you already include in your life to help you live from wellness? How did those come to be so important to you? How is your "plan" working for you overall? What are some new things you'd like to include?

Naming these things—what's working, what's not, and what you'd like to do—can be your way of creating a plan.

The page is an invitation to reflection. The person is an invitation to connection. With a plan, we find our invitation to *intention*.

When we choose intention instead of striving, something new and different emerges, more sustaining than mere achievement, more life-giving than even terrific missional goals. Intention moves us away from a to-do list and into a way of life, immersing us deeper and deeper into the present reality of God, where we will find his energy, wisdom, power, and purposes.

I define a *spiritual practice* as anything I'm intentional about that helps me carve out the time and space to pay attention to, and be responsive to, the ongoing work of God in my life. When we carve out the time and space, we notice and yield to God's presence and action in and around us. So when naming the essentials, I find this to be a helpful framework.

The practice of attention involves attending to the state of our souls: attending to honest realities through reflection, attending to self-awareness through connection, and attending to healthy growth through intention. A page, a person, and a plan.

To be clear, when I started these practices I wasn't consciously implementing some sort of directed, overall plan for my life. Each came to me as I needed them the most and when I had fresh willingness to engage. What I didn't realize—and perhaps couldn't have even hoped for—was that when I leaned into a page, a person, and a plan, I was actually shedding my former anemic under-standing of the human soul and embracing something richer. I was moving into a way of living with God that would change everything for me, allowing me to thrive and flourish, no matter the circumstances of my life.

I was taking on practices that helped me pay attention to God's presence with me in ordinary moments, ordinary conversations, and ordinary routines. These new areas of willingness were giving me the space to discover God in all dimensions of my life. Even when it all burned, I knew how to be rooted to the life beneath the charred soil, and I was equipped with hope that new growth was still to come.

As it turns out, the page, the person, and the plan are just the beginning of the journey toward a healthier soul. There is so much more ahead.

SOUL CARE REFLECTIONS

1. What keeps you from some sort of daily (or near-daily) written reflection? Can you commit to journaling today? This week? Perhaps for thirty days? If you don't already have a journal, choose one and write your first entry.

2. What is the current state of your relationships? Which, if any, are helping you pay attention to God's activity in your life? Set up a time for coffee with a friend or someone in your life you sense is trustworthy. Use this as an opportunity to practice mirroring and self-disclosure, then move into sharing areas of struggle, if appropriate.

3. What elements and steps might help you create a plan
   to move forward with your soul health? For help creating a
   soul care plan, follow the QR code here:

BEYOND SURRENDER

Practicing Participation

In the clamor and din of the day, the press
of Eternity's warm love still whispers in each
of us, as our deepest selves, as our truest
selves. Attend to the Eternal that He may
recreate you and sow you deep into the
furrows of the world's suffering.

THOMAS R. KELLY, *The Eternal Promise*

In one of those early days after the fire, I stood in a cold breeze
at the top of the hill, looking down over the moonlike wasteland
that the valley below had become and realized that I could actually
see all the way down to the bottom of the ravine, down to the dirt
and rocks. Prior to the fires, the hill had been completely overrun.
Over the past hundred years, a green curtain of mature ponderosa
pines had grown thick and impenetrable in places. Tall grasses,
large shrubs, and hordes of prickly pear cactus filled the rest of the
space; if you weren't careful, if you accidentally brushed up against
the wrong plant, some of the plants could do serious harm.

While all those things are beautiful in their own right and
native to this region, they did cut us off from accessing various
parts of the property both visually and, in some cases, physically.

But after the fire, the perspective had changed. When I looked down the hill, I could see all the way down. I could see the ground. I could see the topography of the land. Everything on the surface had been burned, and while it was sad to look at, especially in the context of everything else that had also been destroyed, I realized that something else was going on. I could suddenly see possibilities for the land that I hadn't seen before.

Before the fire, going down to the lower field to clear out all the cactus plants would have been impossible. Now they would be easier to remove because I could see them and navigate around them. I saw opportunities to plant new things down there at the bottom of the hill, envisioned different kinds of crops, began to dream about a place for a barn or structure for outdoor gatherings. Whether or not we had decided to clear the land wasn't the point. For the first time, we were able to see what could be.

Something coming through your life and burning everything around you to the ground is hard and sad. Denying that reality or trying to avoid it isn't just pointless, it's also detrimental. You have to sit in that space and mourn what has been lost. Lament is a vital part of the human experience. But at some point, you'll also need to stand up and look around, take an inventory of your life, and begin examining the possibilities that you could not have seen otherwise. It's easier after the desolation to recognize the spaces in your life that need to be renovated. On the far side of something really hard, we find strange gifts.

If we can survive the fires of our lives and even learn to embrace the desolation, we will begin to see more clearly the potential, the possibilities, the places where we can make changes. Life will look a certain way after this painful thing.

Now that you're building ways of paying attention, what will you be able to see now that you couldn't see before?

SEEING THE UNSEEN

In chapter 1 of the book of Jeremiah, we encounter God asking Jeremiah an unusual question. He's preparing Jeremiah for the prophetic work ahead of him, and twice in that first chapter, in verses 11 and 13, God asks the same question: "What do you see?"

The things that Jeremiah sees ("the branch of an almond tree" [v. 11] and "a pot that is boiling . . . tilting toward us from the north" [v. 13]) form a kind of foundation for all that Jeremiah will see and do for the rest of the book as he takes on the role of prophet to the people of God. Jeremiah is learning to see accurately into the unseen and then to speak about what he sees. That's why the question is so important. He will see, hear, and speak for God.

What do you see, Jeremiah?

For me, the land after the fires became a time for seeing things differently. I felt the Spirit within me inviting a similar question: *Mindy, what do you see?*

Because of the new vision we receive directly following times of difficulty, because of what we can now see that we couldn't see before, our Gardens of Desolation often prove to be the hinge points between the seen and the unseen.

Times when our openness to what God might be doing increases.

Times when we might even lean disproportionately into the reality of the unseen world.

Times when everything changes.

Where our lives go following a crisis of any kind is not a given.

Our openness to that unseen realm and our attentiveness to it often depends on the state of our souls, or at least on our willingness to consider what state our souls are in.

When I look back at 1995, and then again at 2021, the complete destruction I experienced during both times brought my life down to its foundation. All excess activities, desires, responsibilities, and relationships were suspended or removed. But the second time, I had language, willingness, and an imagination that helped me stay connected to God's presence. In both cases, as I clung to that unseen reality moment by moment, day by day, I began building again. And what God's Spirit built along with me in the succeeding years was something that never could have existed without that experience of desolation.

I think the life we're invited into, this life of soul care, is very much about becoming hinge-point people, people who can operate even in places of desolation, whether that desolation occurs in our own lives or in the lives of others. We don't completely despair, and we don't run away from sitting with others in that space where they are suffering. Hinge-point people know the gifts available in a Garden of Desolation and what they can bring into our lives.

This seen-and-unseen space is what Jesus called the Kingdom of Heaven, the Here and Now alongside the Not Yet. We are invited, during these difficult moments especially, to sit at that intersection, that hinge point where the two worlds intertwine. We remain deeply engaged in the here and now—and yet also deeply connected to the unseen reality of God. In that place, we lean forward with anticipation and surrender, stepping into our lives as agents of the Kingdom who are alert to the confluence.

Particularly when we are surrounded by pain or suffering, when we've sat in the Garden of Desolation and waded through our grief, it can be easy to believe that all that matters is what can be seen. That's where we get our strong, learned bias to get back to work, wipe away or ignore our tears, and stand up and take back control of the situation.

But if we're going to be hinge-point people, we can't go back to that. Taking back control means reverting to the busy, striving, controlling life we lived before the breakdown or the burnout or the fire. To take back control, to move forward without centering ourselves in the Kingdom, means ignoring the hinge point into the unseen and once again living, or attempting to live, an entirely self-directed life in our own strength. We'll miss the gift of receiving our lives and orientation from something more profound and more real than all that can be seen.

The Kingdom of God is more real than these words you are reading, more real than the chair you're sitting on. The unseen goodness and reality of God undergirds, permeates, and supersedes everything we can see and touch and taste and hear and smell. And the unseen reality of God and the rightness of God's ways, or character, is what ultimately undergirds a healthy soul. Our souls find great rest, or "perfect peace" (Isaiah 26:3), in that unseen reality. No matter how disturbed or chaotic our lives might be in what can be seen, we can enter into these circumstances with a kind of lightness, increasingly anchoring ourselves to the unseen reality of God, where we can trust that all is fundamentally well.

BECOMING A HINGE-POINT PERSON

I enjoy considering how all that transpired around the birth of Jesus was a sneaky move to bring the Messiah into the kingdom of the earth on the down-low—a key leader placed behind enemy lines to be raised up in an unsuspecting place and in unsuspecting ways. With no big announcements, no fanfare, the Son of God is born as a helpless infant among the lowly and poor.

The interplay between what is going on in the seen and the unseen is dramatic in the story of Advent:

- In the seen, an unmarried teenager becomes pregnant, and her fiancé decides to go through with the marriage and raising of this child. In the seen, a few angels show up with some pretty remarkable reports about what is happening in the unseen.

- In the unseen, Jesus arrives precisely where he needs to be, as was foretold by the prophets, so that his life will reestablish his Kingdom rule and reign on the earth. In the unseen, the final death blow to death itself has been set in motion.

What I see in this story as well, though, are hinge-point people. People whose posture of surrender allows God's unfolding purposes in the unseen to collide precisely with what is happening in the seen.

Mary and Joseph stood at the uncomfortable, illogical intersection of the seen and the unseen. Mary in particular was willing to exist at that sometimes-painful confluence of the Not Yet and the Here and Now. Her story unfolds in hidden, secret, impossible ways.

You probably know the story well. An angel appears to Mary and says,

"Greetings, you who are highly favored! The Lord is with you."

Mary was greatly troubled at his words and wondered what kind of greeting this might be. But the angel said to her, "Do not be afraid, Mary; you have found favor with God. You will conceive and give birth to a son, and you are to call him Jesus. He will be great and will be called the Son of the Most High. The Lord God will give him the throne of his father David, and he will reign over Jacob's descendants forever; his kingdom will never end."

"How will this be," Mary asked the angel, "since I am a virgin?"

The angel answered, "The Holy Spirit will come on you, and the power of the Most High will overshadow you. So the holy one to be born will be called the Son of God. Even Elizabeth your relative is going to have a child in her old age, and she who was said to be unable to conceive is in her sixth month. For no word from God will ever fail."

"I am the Lord's servant," Mary answered. "May your word to me be fulfilled." Then the angel left her.
LUKE 1:28-38

Talk about finding yourself at the ultimate hinge point! God coming to earth in human flesh! And what is Mary's response when presented with the part she will play in this monumental move? She accepts her role as a servant of God and then adds her willing assent: asking that all the angel has said would be fulfilled.

Certainly the part of the drama Mary was invited into was historic and one of a kind. But God is still at work in our world, redeeming and restoring and rescuing and healing and guiding and preserving. God is active. Today, right now. And God continues to invite each and every one of us into the same unfolding drama, whether through an angel or through the unfolding of circumstances.

How will we respond? Can we, when God reveals an opportunity to us—perhaps even a difficult one—be like Mary in our response?

"May your word to me be fulfilled."

Can we posture ourselves in quiet surrender as we are invited into the unfolding drama between what is seen and what is unseen—as God's Kingdom rule is yet being revealed on earth as it is in heaven?

That is what marks the life of hinge-point people.

Becoming and remaining attuned to the interplay between the Not Yet and the Here and Now of the Kingdom requires stepping into a lifestyle of surrender. We take on a yielded way of being. Not only are we not creating our own agendas, we're actually giving up our own agendas, anchoring our confidence in God and not in our own strength.

Yes, in the seen we have many dangers, toils, and snares. We grow concerned about what will happen or what the outcomes of various situations will be. But God wants us to experience the world beyond what we can see, hear, touch, taste, and smell. God invites us to live out of a deep and grounded knowledge that the Kingdom of God and what happens there somehow supersedes the pain, fear, and ugliness that are so commonplace in the world.

But, with that said, we cannot only choose surrender when we occasionally and unintentionally visit the Garden of Desolation.

Soul care cultivates dependence and surrender as a way of life, no matter the circumstance. It's a lifestyle in which we gladly train ourselves to remain fixed on Jesus and take our cues from what is happening in the unseen rather than in the seen.

I was praying along these lines before a big meeting recently. I was excited and wanted the outcome to line up with my hopes and dreams, but I also understood that I couldn't possibly know what outcome would be best for me. I can't see the future. I can't see the ends of all possible timelines. Remembering this helps me stay in a posture of surrender and openness. Yes, I show up and create and lead and take next steps in the seen, but my posture, usually on a daily basis, is to remind myself to surrender.

We all have our lists of what we're hoping for or afraid of, but continuing to connect with that unseen reality of the Kingdom of God allows us to send out our antennae a little further to pick up more than what we can see. We don't know what's going to happen tomorrow or what conversations are happening at this very moment that might be impacting outcomes we care about. Certainly in Mary's life, as Jesus' mother, there were many points of suffering and pain (Luke 2:35), but the final outcome was joy. Who could have foreseen it? No one but the unseen God. (And so we must circle back to dependence. Trusting that God knows the outcomes allows us to trust in what we cannot see.)

Thomas R. Kelly, in his book *A Testament of Devotion*, writes:

> Life is meant to be lived from a Center, a divine Center.
> . . . Life from the Center is a life of unhurried peace
> and power. It is simple. It is serene. It is amazing. It is
> triumphant. It is radiant. It takes no time, but it occupies
> all our time. And it makes our life programs new and

overcoming. We need not get frantic. He is at the helm. And when our little day is done we lie down quietly in peace, for all is well.[1]

In a life of quiet surrender, we are not robots, but our posture presumes that we are involved with God in what is being done on earth as it is in heaven. And not only with God but, importantly, in the *way* of God. We walk in peace, contentment, joy, perseverance. We develop the ability to endure suffering. And we can only experience this when we live from the divine Center.

Can we imagine a future suffused with God's involvement, where all will be well?

THE MIND OF GOD

We get to operate as representatives, agents, messengers, embodied bringers of the unseen life and purposes of God into the realm of the seen. In many ways, that's the most exciting part of living from soul health: being able—truly able—to join in God's activity in and around us!

But often we wonder, *How do I know I'm operating correctly on God's behalf?* Presuming upon God in the right ways but not the wrong ways? I've seen it happen too many times in my life and in the lives of others: Lacking humility, we speak of something we confidently believe to be God's will only to find that what we've said does not happen or work out in any way that could be considered good.

I certainly don't have the answers on this, but an experience with my son Jonathan gave me a glimpse of how this *could* work.

When Jonathan was in college, he called me one afternoon

while I was in a meeting. The timing of his call was fairly unusual, so I excused myself from the meeting and answered as I walked the historic tree-lined streets of Mapleton Hill behind my office. As I walked, I could see between the trees the iconic Flatirons heralding the front range of the Rocky Mountains, towering above the small city of Boulder.

Why had Jonathan interrupted my day at work? What was so important? Well, for whatever forgotten reason, he had my credit card. We live in the same city, so it isn't that unusual—sometimes he runs errands as a favor to me or makes a payment on my behalf at the dentist's office.

But this day, he called to tell me he had decided to use my credit card *without asking me first*. He didn't want me to be surprised when I saw the transaction on my bank app—but, he explained, he had used it to buy around $120 of food for a gathering of Young Life leaders he served alongside.

"I just wanted to tell you I did this," he said. "I knew it was something you would be glad to pay for."

As I was walking up the hill while we spoke, I got hit by a wave of the unseen. I sensed God speaking: *That's what it looks like to trust in my will in a matter and move in confidence—when you know my heart about a particular thing, and you use my resources to accomplish purposes you know are aligned with me.*

It felt bizarrely reassuring, and somewhat like being loved, to have one of my kids say they spent some of my money to do something they knew I'd be excited about. He used his own judgment and initiative, and in the action he took, he actually made me feel loved and known.

Julian of Norwich once said, "For God wishes to be seen, and he wishes to be sought, and he wishes to be expected, and he wishes to be trusted."[2] And in that moment I caught a glimpse of how this might feel to God. How God desires to be expected. I was so grateful that Jonathan had used that money in the way he had. Jonathan knew the mind of Mindy. He knew the mind of Mindy would be happy to toss that money toward pizza for Young Life leaders. He knew the resources were there. My intent or will had been known, and he had confidence I would respond in a certain way.

When we have that kind of relationship with God, we can move ahead with confidence even in the mystery. We can make requests of God's resources to meet various needs and opportunities we encounter along the way. Out of love and relationship, we are to step into our local contexts paying attention to what God intends around the world.

Hinge-point people do more than simply share the mind of God; we use that oneness to shape our actions and interactions with the world around us.

Hannah Hurnard, who authored *Hinds' Feet on High Places*, writes in her book *God's Transmitters* that, as God's children, we have become conductive material, one hand holding to God and the other holding whatever circumstances we are in. The clear teaching of Jesus' invitation to prayer suggests that what we transmit in this exchange is nothing less than God's goodness, power, love, and mercy. Often, we transmit God's Kingdom to the Here and Now world when we pay attention to ideas that the Spirit places in our minds. Oftentimes we have no way of knowing where these ideas come from; they seem to come from nowhere!

After the fires, a neighbor suggested that we gather virtually to support one another as a community—and out of seemingly nowhere I had one of those maybe-it's-the-Spirit ideas: I could host those kinds of calls so they wouldn't be limited to the free forty minutes included with a basic Zoom membership. I gathered the emails and invited a growing list of neighbors, most of whom I'd never met since we were new to the area. We began hosting a space where people could check in, find out news about any government and nonprofit services becoming available, offer each other information about insurance and contractors, and provide encouragement in the complete chaos after the fires. Some neighbors were living in hotel rooms with three kids, two dogs, and a cat, trying to hold down their virtual jobs. Some were holed up in unfurnished rental units just trying to find mugs for morning coffee. Some left town and stayed with family members as they tried to navigate salvage and repairs from a distance. We were all trying to understand the risks of toxicity from smoke damage and soot in walls, lawns, carpets, insulation, and neighborhood playgrounds. When firewood burns, that's one thing. When refrigerators and clothing and window treatments and carpets and mattresses and roof shingles burn, that's an entirely different story. There were frequent tears over insurance coverage limitations and facing moves back into houses potentially still full of toxic chemicals.

We didn't have any agenda for the calls—we just wanted to offer a place where everyone could process what had happened with the wildfires and talk about where they were on their road to recovery. And these Zoom calls became way more popular than I ever could have imagined! We started meeting every other day.

One day, while taking a call from our former home's driveway because our Wi-Fi at the house still worked, my husband, Jeff, followed a prompting from the Spirit to talk with a man driving a service vehicle that kept circling our former neighborhood. It turns out that man was Captain Jamie Wood, who had led a cohort of five different firefighting teams called into our neighborhood the night of the fire. As a wildfire specialist, Captain Wood had worked all over the US, but he lived locally. He had never before returned to an area he'd defended. He and his team were the primary group responsible for saving our house and the portions of our neighborhood that hadn't been completely destroyed. We learned many details about the night of the fire because Jeff got out of his car to meet this man in our neighborhood in the days after the fire.

Because of those God-whispered connections, we were able to invite Captain Wood to one of the neighborhood Zoom calls. Talk about a holy moment! He openly wept as he retold the firefighting stories from that day and night, when they finally left our neighborhood at two thirty in the morning to continue the fight on another front, the fire still smoldering though its progression had stopped. Person after person, neighbor after neighbor on that Zoom call thanked him over and over again for all he had done. Many of us were able to thank him for the work that saved our homes. Several joined the call who had lost their homes, and they, too, through their tears, thanked him. Everyone understood that if the firefighters hadn't stopped to defend our street, the unique open space behind our homes would have allowed the fires to progress into the center of Louisville and damage hundreds more structures and the historic town center. Naming that together was a tender, beautiful thing.

I tell you all this to encourage you. Hopefully your context won't involve such loss and tragedy. But when we open ourselves up to the signals being sent from God, when we respond to the various promptings of the Spirit to initiate and love people, God often uses that space to facilitate connection and healing. People knew of my faith and association with our local church, but those Zoom calls weren't necessarily Godward focused. Even so, God did use our responsiveness to create space for community in the middle of devastation.

PARTICIPATING WITH GOD

When we find ourselves at life's hinge points, prepared to surrender our own agendas and become part of the Kingdom movement in our world, something interesting can happen.

We can move beyond simple surrender and into a participatory life with God.

Dallas Willard beautifully illustrates this point in ten or so paragraphs buried at the core of his book *Renovation of the Heart*. He speaks of moving through four phases of spiritual development: surrender, abandonment, contentment, and participation.[3]

While *surrender* is a deep reality that persists in the life of the new Christian, Willard says it's akin to arguing with God about something and then being figuratively pinned to the ground in a wrestling match until we give up the fight. Early in our lives as Christ followers, the Kingdom doesn't make much sense to us, and it takes God graciously forcing our hands before we will surrender. Willard would say this level of surrender is not a reflection of deep partnership and trust but rather a kind of spiritual immaturity. It's certainly nothing to be ashamed of since it's a natural phase of moving closer to God. However, only turning toward God once all other options have been exhausted is not a posture one should maintain for one's entire life.

Willard identifies the next stage as *abandonment*, and this is when we begin to have a strong sense of what makes sense to

God, especially in our own lives and the world around us. We have a better understanding of who God is, and the gap between how we see the world and how God sees the world begins to diminish. We yield more readily to God's will, we don't have to get pinned down to the ground, and we're much more trusting of God and his ways. Maybe I don't have to have the last word in an argument, or maybe I'm more willing to give my resources to someone in need, even if neither of those things yet feels very natural to me. The way of Jesus may still feel unnatural, but I am learning how that way can be trusted. I can see the path of Jesus and abandon myself more readily to that way. Perhaps in this phase, I begin overriding my natural tendencies. I choose to pray for enemies, love unconditionally, and bless those who harm me—all things that previously didn't make any sense, and for the most part still don't—but I abandon myself to the rightness of that path. Abandonment is more confident of God and his ways than mere surrender.

As we move further along this continuum of relationship and trust, the reality of the Kingdom increasingly becomes the air we breathe, the source of our lives. We're drawing from something entirely different than we were when we were simply surrendering or even choosing to abandon ourselves to God's ways. Willard refers to this third phase as *contentment*. Here, no matter what happens, good or bad, we can say, "It is well, because I am held by God." And we don't say it with gritted teeth, but rather we speak out of our lived experience—it's what our reality truly looks like. The unseen has begun to overshadow the seen. This is the peace that transcends understanding. This kind of radical contentment is available whether we have a ton of stuff or no stuff, whether people love us or hate us, and truly, though it sounds extreme, whether we live or die. We remain anchored in God, content. We're breathing different air.

The capacities for flourishing in these stages are enormous because here we engage directly with the Kingdom. We no longer derive our sense of well-being only from the here-and-now circumstances that surround us. We can be—and in fact are—fundamentally well, no matter what.

As we journey from surrender to abandonment to contentment, we finally enter what Willard calls *participation*. We become freely and lightly aligned with God and completely yielded to his purposes in and around us, gratefully releasing our own agendas and remaining alert to God's agenda, God's activity, at the intersection of the seen and the unseen. This way of relating to God is what the mystics referred to as union: We become one with him, and yet we do not lose our identity in that immersion. Now we are most fully alive and most fully who God uniquely created us to be.

In this place, when God says jump, we're jumping and asking how high as we go, yielded to what God is saying in that moment and completely trusting in whatever outcome God causes to come about. There's an excitement, too, because we've seen what God has done in our lives when we've surrendered and abandoned our own way, and we can't wait to see where God leads us next. Even further—and this is mind-blowing—God welcomes our ideas and our initiative as we move out into the needs and opportunities of the world, bringing the ways and resources of the unseen into the seen.

Participation is how we can become hinge-point people. God's people scattered all over the world are not as two billion vacuous robots but sentient, creative, imaginative, powerful partners in bringing about the Kingdom on earth as it is in heaven.

This is the kind of life I want to live. And I think it's the kind of life where, as Jesus' people, we experience the most in terms of hope and joy, delighting in those around us. Hard things still happen to us, but even when they do, we stay at the hinge point, anchored both to the pain of real life and to the ultimate reality of the unseen. We experience our difficulties as invitations into curiosity, to explore what is or might be happening.

In participation, even when we see no "solution" to our pain and suffering, we recognize and embrace a redemptive arc taking place within it. We know, too, the unseen reality of a redemptive arc in the pain and suffering of the wider world, in which God doesn't demonstrate power so much in preventing evil but in transforming it.

How can the pain in each of our lives—the suffering, the mistakes, the abuse, the harm that came our way—activate our imaginations to seek out the ways that God is redeeming the story?

How do we show up as our own true selves in history, alive to our own journeys but also alive to God's movement in and around our journeys? And how does that empower us as transmitters, walking in the way of Jesus and in the supernatural guidance of God even as we can't control or predict where God is leading us?

When we are able to imagine ways we can be hinge-point people, we begin moving beyond simple surrender and enter into the excitement of participation with God in the beautiful, regenerative, and transformational things taking place in the seen and the unseen. That imagination doesn't just tend to our souls, it also motivates and energizes us to be alive in a wholly new way.

SOUL CARE REFLECTIONS

1. Are you sitting in a place of desolation right now? Is the desolation your own pain or someone else's? How might the reality of the Kingdom of Heaven intersect this space?

2. Think of an area in your life where there has been significant loss or failure or devastation. Prayerfully survey that part of your life and begin to open your heart to questions. What can you now see that you couldn't see before? What is suddenly possible in your life that could never have been possible before the destruction occurred?

3. Which of Dallas Willard's phases seems to best describe your own life these days—surrender, abandonment, contentment, or participation? What might living from an even stronger confidence in God open up for you? Share about the phases with a friend or someone you trust and ask which phase they think they're in.

4. Consider the evils or tragedies or injustices that have captivated your heart or mind. What kind of improvements do you imagine might be possible? What strategies? What resources? What teams? What technology? What innovation?

CULTIVATING HEALTHY SOUL SOIL

Practicing Delight

If more of us valued food and cheer and song
above hoarded gold, it would be a merrier world.

THORIN IN J. R. R. TOLKIEN'S *The Hobbit*

"What would give you joy, Mindy? What's something that would
be fun for you to do?"

Jeff's question stopped me in my tracks. As I thought about
my answer—and struggled to come up with one—I felt a sort of
panic set in. At the time, we had no expendable income, no extra
money lying around for a rainy day. We were planting a church
and raising a family, and my major medical incident was barely
a year in the rearview. I didn't think I had the luxury of time or
resources to do something fun.

The harder truth was that I didn't really even know what I
enjoyed doing anymore. Years and years of driven living had forced
out all the hobbies and simple, seemingly purposeless pleasures I

might have pursued. Who had time for a hobby? Who had time to do things simply for enjoyment?

"I really don't know," I replied. "Maybe I don't know how to have fun."

"Well, what would be life-giving to you?" he persisted.

I began to dig deep into my memories. *When did I feel joy? When did I feel truly alive?* Finally, something came to my mind. "I might enjoy horseback riding," I said.

Horseback riding. I hadn't thought about that for decades. Riding horses was something I had loved as a kid. The feeling of being carried by something so powerful, of riding trails and galloping across open fields. But there hadn't really been a good reason, or extra time, for me to keep doing it beyond a few trail rides here and there over the years.

Then Jeff insisted, "You should do that. You should go horseback riding."

So, despite our circumstances, I arranged for a few hours of horseback riding. My detailed feelings of emotional discomfort that day are almost easier to remember than the actual experience of riding the horse. Sitting in the parking lot, I debated whether I was actually going to go through with it.

I shouldn't be here. This is costing too much money. We had to arrange for someone to watch the kids. The kids—how are they doing? Maybe I should just go home.

But in those days, I was crawling my way back to a new life— and Jeff was gently insisting, even in the face of all my concerns and hesitations and doubts, that I simply do something for the enjoyment of it. That didn't make sense to me, but I had landed myself in a world of hurt by doing what had made sense to me for so many years. So I listened. I did it. I rode a horse.

Then, not too many years in the future, a woman in our small group in Chicago found out that I loved to ride horses. She and her husband had a barn full of horses, and she invited me over. As it turned out, these were no ordinary barn horses. She had several notable breeds, including a few thoroughbreds—powerful, intelligent, spirited animals.

Over the years, she and I would ride out—not single file like on a typical trail ride, but side by side—through autumn leaves and fresh snow, wide fields and deep creeks, broad hillsides and narrow, wooded trails. Surrounded by silence but for our occasional conversation and the sound of hooves striking the rocks and thudding on the earth, I was grateful for the gift of riding and building a friendship at the same time.

One day, I had the opportunity to ride one of the thoroughbreds—and for the first time, we took to the track. It was around nine in the morning, and the sun was low and hazy in the sky. I did several loops with my mare, Shannon, around the track, each time increasing both her speed and my confidence.

Then it happened, the sight that nearly took my breath away. As I came flying around the western long side of the track, the sun shining low in the eastern sky, I looked down to my left. There, perfectly silhouetted, was a clear shadow: Shannon, her mane and tail flying in the wind of a full gallop; me, motionlessly crouched on her back . . . flying!

That moment was one of the most beautiful and energizing things I had ever seen or experienced, a glorious snapshot of a larger experience of delight. Whether I'm mucking out stalls or riding trails or, yes, maybe especially, flying on the back of a thoroughbred, I notice my soul coming alive when I'm around horses—even the horses I pass by on my drive into Boulder these days.

The experience of delight is good for my soul. And I think God delights in my delighting.

ESSENTIAL DELIGHT

Some of us naturally lean toward the idea of delight.

Some of us struggle to know where to begin.

Several years back, a friend and I shared the teaching responsibilities for a three-city tour with a women's event called Breathe. My friend taught the main content, and then I facilitated some questions based on her message. As part of her message, my friend shared about giving herself permission to return to supposedly useless things that she had enjoyed as a child—picking up an instrument that had remained silent for years, reengaging in creative endeavors, those sorts of things. It was a way of breathing fresh life into her weary soul.

In each gathering, I had given the hundreds of women in attendance an assignment: "List six things that give you joy, and then turn to the person next to you and share your list." That was it. Simple, right? Six things that give you joy. Could be a color, a favorite food, riding a horse, playing the flute, anything!

In each city, this produced some brief reflection and writing in a notebook, followed by laughter and energetic conversation. But in the third city we visited, I noticed a very different dynamic in the room.

This time, when I asked the question, I heard a series of audible gasps—and then a hush fell over the room. No one knew what to say. I asked them what in their lives brings them joy, and they had no idea.

As it turned out, we later learned that this was a context with a more conservative and even restrictive view of women's roles. It seems that somehow, in the midst of that context, these women had lost their capacity for delight.

They're not the only ones. Many of us don't even know what brings us joy anymore. For certain personality types, it's hard for us to do something we love when it doesn't seem "useful." But the pursuit of joy is actually very serious business.

What brings life to you? What gives you a sense of delight? Do you make time for those activities?

If you struggle to answer those questions, I get it. But I believe that the experience of delight is something we must pursue if we want to care for the health of our souls.

As children, we hold a deep desire and capacity to experience delight and joy. I distinctly remember, as a kid, sitting at the back of church for three-hour worship services on Saturday nights, feeling amazed at the music, the passion, the emotion. My childlike faith and desire for God were caught up in wonder and delight.

One of the songs we often sang in that church included a line that I loved: *The joy of the Lord is my strength.* Those words come from the book of Nehemiah:

> Nehemiah the governor, Ezra the priest and teacher of the Law, and the Levites who were instructing the people said to them all, "This day is holy to the Lord your God. Do not mourn or weep." For all the people had been weeping as they listened to the words of the Law.

Nehemiah said, "Go and enjoy choice food and
sweet drinks, and send some to those who have nothing
prepared. This day is holy to our Lord. Do not grieve,
for the joy of the Lord is your strength."
NEHEMIAH 8:9-10

Do not grieve, for the joy of the Lord is your strength.

My dad and I painted the musical score from that song in
my room, just above my grandmother's black upright Wurlitzer.
(Getting my own room was a rare treat—there were five of us at
the time, but I was the only girl, so I got my own space.)

As we get older, though, the trials and sadness of the world
make joy seem like a pipe dream, right? We put delight into a
category of something we can never truly experience, at least not
on a regular basis. We feel like unless we can attach some kind of
utilitarian value to things that simply delight us, those things are
probably nonessential.

But delight is what we're made for. Joy is how our brains function best.[1]

Neurotheologian Dr. Jim Wilder makes the following observation about joy:

From a brain perspective, joy stimulates the growth of the
brain systems involved in character formation, identity
consolidation, and moral behavior.[2]

That is to say, we actually become better people when we are
living with a sense of joy. How would our family dynamics change
if we made more time in our schedules for delight? What would
our teenagers' lives be like? Who would we all become?

Jesus gave joy as the reason for his teaching in John 15:11 and the central feature of his prayer for disciples in John 17:13.[3]

Jesus said, "These things have I spoken unto you, that my joy might remain in you, and that your joy might be full" (John 15:11, KJV). In other words, he spent all that time teaching the disciples not simply so they would know things but so they would find their joy in him! What an incredible concept, that his teachings were meant to inspire delight and joy in his followers!

Joy is equally powerful when we are in painful states.[4]

When we are suffering and a friend comes to us and puts their arms around us, Wilder says, what we feel in that instant, despite the pain, is true joy. Isn't it amazing that we feel joy even in the midst of heartbreak? "Someone is with us, and we are not alone."[5] Someone loves us! There is joy to be found even in the most difficult circumstances, and it often—usually?—comes to us in the form of presence: the presence of a friend or a family member, and the presence of the Holy Spirit.

Too often we forget that joy is available to us anytime, anywhere. When we're confused or sad or lonely or afraid, true joy can carry us through. Delight must be something we keep coming back to, continually return to.

How do we return to joy even when life is hard?

When I'm noticing a lack of joy in my own life, I heed Dr. Wilder's advice and call to mind that God is with me, no matter what. And beyond the fact that God is with me, I find it helpful to remember that God is glad to be with me. He's not just tolerating me. I suspect that even in challenging times, God is delighted to be with me—and with you.

One way I stay joyful is by thinking about joy even in the midst of hard things. So if I'm in the middle of a difficult meeting, or receiving news I didn't want, or walking away from a tough conversation with a friend or family member, I remind myself that I can be joyful even then. And it's not about pretending hard things aren't happening; it's about realizing that joy can fill in the little spaces in all of life's moments, even the hard times.

Another way I return to joy is by remembering the reality of the invisible Kingdom all around me. No matter the circumstances of my life, I have the ability to put my hope and trust in an unseen God who is working in ways I cannot understand for my good: "So we fix our eyes not on what is seen, but on what is unseen" (2 Corinthians 4:18).

God is constantly working, without ceasing, no matter the state of my soul. Knowing that I cannot even fathom all the various good things going on all around me—that brings me to joy.

Finally, I try to keep little mementos in my life that remind me of joy. One example of this is my collection of little sparrow figurines. To me, the sparrow is the visible symbol of an unseen reality, that I'm being cared for by a God whose eye is even on the sparrow (see Matthew 10:29-31). This helps me return to joy.

THE SPIRITUAL PRACTICE OF DELIGHT

Sometimes spiritual practices are positioned in a way that communicates, "Do these things, and you'll feel less anxious!" or "Do these things, and your relationship issues will improve!" And in some ways, sure, it's true. Can delight help us endure suffering? Yes. Does joy help us experience peace? Yes. Does grounding ourselves in what brings life help us let go of our fears, doubts, and insecurities? Yes.

But—I hope you're catching on to this—there's a bigger picture here. Pursuing delight does help keep our soul health from falling apart, but even more exciting and compelling than that is what God can do with a healthy soul energized by joy: With it, we end up being agents of healing, change, and restoration. We become joy bringers not only in our own lives but also in the lives of those around us.

The hope of spiritual formation for the Christian is that over time we are being shaped into the likeness and image of Jesus. Anything good that comes from doing any of the practices we've talked about so far is not thanks to our own strength or imagination. If we are taking credit for the good that comes from spiritual practices, we are actually separating ourselves from God instead of growing closer to him and his purposes. That's it. That's the foundation for why we practice things like silent prayer or surrender or solitude. That's why we practice generosity or celebration or Bible study. It's all to become shaped into the likeness and image of Jesus. The practical outworking of a spiritual practice is that it changes what we see—because when we see the right things, really notice them, it changes how we live. This is the promise of spiritual formation.

When I've been practicing delight and I see opposition, lack, injustice, or pain in the world around me, I don't make my approach with white knuckles and anxiety, trying to remember how to be a Christian in the midst of all that while also being a force for good in the world. Instead, delight helps me effortlessly see what a child of God would do in the midst of this world's brokenness.

God is the source of joy (Proverbs 8:30-31). The fruit of the Spirit includes joy (Galatians 5:22). So, when our souls are healthy, fed by God through the practice of various spiritual disciplines, we respond without even thinking in ways that reflect the Holy Spirit—responses that often include joy.

I think this is a much more compelling reason for pursuing our own spiritual formation. It's not simply to do things that make me feel better or give me a more balanced life. Rather, it's to do things that open me up to transformation, into the character, or way, or likeness of Christ. As I interact with the world in all its goodness and all its problems, I more naturally see and participate in bringing God's solutions to bear.

THE PRACTICE IS THE MISSION

The year was 1999. I had just started this baby organization called Soul Care, and I was feeling overwhelmed . . . again. I was an elder, a mother of three kids, involved in a fledgling little church, and I found myself in the car one day, driving who knows where, complaining to God about my life.

Which of these am I supposed to do, God? These are all really big things! Am I supposed to be launching Young Life in this region? Really digging in and helping at church? Forging ahead with Soul Care? Simply caring for my family? What is it you want me to do?

Then I heard, inaudibly but as clear as anything, Jesus ask me a question: *What do you want to do?* In other words, *What would delight you the most?*

Oh, that made me mad! It didn't seem fair. I didn't want to

decide what to keep doing and what to give up! I just wanted God to tell me what direction to go, what would have the greatest impact in the world, what he was working out for me to do. After all, isn't that what the Bible promises?

> We know that in all things God works for the good of
> those who love him, who have been called according to
> his purpose.
> **ROMANS 8:28**

Most of us are familiar with how the New International Version translates this verse. But if you think about it, these words frame our role in God's work as fairly passive. God is busy in the background, working everything out. He's even the one who has called us, while we just make sure we love him.

But the footnotes in the NIV give us an alternate rendering, turning our usual understanding of this verse on its head. What if, at the heart, this is what Romans 8:28 really means?

> We know that in all things God works together with
> those who love him to bring about what is good—with
> those who have been called according to his purpose.

That's different, right? These words place us on our tiptoes, to lean in and work together with God to bring about what is good.

God is actively at work in the world. And God has chosen to work—largely—through human beings. You and me and every other person on the planet who loves him.

God is interested in our desire and our involvement. God prefers that we work together with him, work together with our brothers and sisters in Christ, because of the indwelling Holy Spirit that lives in all of us, active all around the world. And what motivates our desire, our involvement? A sense of obligation? A gritty determination to do what we're supposed to?

I don't know about you, but that sounds a lot like striving all over again.

The question God asked me is so often what Jesus asked those he encountered in the New Testament:

What do you want?

What do you want me to do for you?

What are you seeking?

When we're not sure what to do with our lives, Jesus is standing there, saying, "I placed you in this unique situation—only you, out of everyone in the entire world. Now go think, and relate with others, and imagine what the Kingdom might look like here on earth."

Imagine, for a moment, that God is asking this of you.

What do you want?

Making space for delight in your life might be the very thing that brings awareness of where God is leading you to interact with the world. As we talked about earlier, surrender is only the entry point for those of us who have decided to follow Christ. Participation is the ultimate calling. And though we might want God to step in and give us a list of the things to be done, in reality God is putting his arm around us and asking, *What do you want? . . . In what do you delight?*

SOUL CARE REFLECTIONS

1. What are a few things that bring you delight?

2. Plan to do something this week for the sheer enjoyment of doing it. What will you do? How much time will you dedicate to doing this?

3. Have you ever encountered God while simply enjoying something or delighting in something?

4. Is it difficult for you to believe that your life as a follower of Christ might not only be about sacrifice and perseverance but also about delight and enjoyment?

5. Write about the people in your life who are doing Kingdom work and who seem to be enjoying themselves immensely. Have a conversation with them about this.

SHY AND FEARLESS

Practicing Humility

Your patient has become humble; have you drawn
his attention to the fact? All virtues are less formidable
to us once the man is aware that he has them, but this
is specially true of humility.
SCREWTAPE IN C. S. LEWIS'S *The Screwtape Letters*

"How big is your platform?"

Have you ever heard that question? In our age of influencers
and social media clout, platform has become a way of determin-
ing a person's importance, relevance, ability to impact others. The
metrics of platform are things like how many Instagram followers you have, how many likes you get on a post, or how large
your email list has become. Our sense of worth can be tied to our
numbers.

Even if you're not in a traditional position of leadership, the
pull of platform can be very real. It is easy to become anxious
over whether anyone has commented on your social media post.
Measuring our worth by our personal visibility has become a very
real concern for people in all walks of life.

How big is your platform?

The same conversation about platform extends to the church, too, with a leader's credibility often conflated with their visibility. I sometimes wonder if this is a necessary part of ministry today or if it's something that only serves the ego. What would spiritual leaders like Henri Nouwen or Dallas Willard have done had they started ministering and writing today? Would they have had smartphones, IG accounts, blue checks by their ~~Twitter~~ X handles? Would they have even become well-known voices to begin with?

It's hard to say if their quiet, gentle voices would have made it above the fray.

Human nature being what it is, I suppose that every generation has used some kind of metric to measure worth. How many people have cited your research? How much capital did you raise for your start-up? How many cattle do you own? How many people work for you? How large is your army?

And now the measure of our worth can be viewed by how nice our last vacation was or how delicious the meal looked or how impressive the birthday party for our two-year-old was. Maybe we want to exaggerate our follower count, or maybe we want our family to look much happier than we really are. Whenever metrics set the agenda, the temptation to inflate the truth follows.

After a while, in some settings, I've nearly come to expect it.

Recently, I found myself in a conversation with the new point leader of an organization I'd started working with. As we began discussing their marketing reach, I had a certain set of expectations. Based on my prior experience with these kinds of organizations, inflated metrics were bound to show up.

When I asked how many people were on their email list, she

immediately replied, "Oh, around seventy thousand," which I took to be pretty strong! I then asked how engaged that audience is, and she acknowledged that she wasn't sure quite yet. In fact, she went on to tell me that the actual email list number was ninety thousand but she felt compelled to lower the number to something she'd felt more accurately reflected the list's potential.

When she said *the mailing list is actually ninety thousand*, I was shocked.

Wait.

What?

If you've never interacted with someone on metrics tied to their perceived success or performance, trust me on this: A leader never *intentionally* understates their numbers. The earned reputation of many leaders is that they exaggerate—sometimes a lot! There's a tendency among many ministry leaders to exaggerate the numbers of their church or baptisms or small groups or serving teams. It has earned a nickname: "pastor math." Most would have anchored that list size at ninety thousand and then likely rounded up to at least one hundred thousand to make it sound just a little better, just a little more impressive. Some might have bumped it higher still!

But this leader had intentionally undersold the size of her email list because she wanted to give me a more accurate sense of their subscribers' engagement. Her goal was to reflect the truth with humility.

In my American context, we don't tend to be known for our humility. It doesn't matter if we are pastors or business leaders, stay-at-home moms or teachers: We are all presented with the temptation to make things look more impressive than they really are. And this lack of humility reveals something about the soul of our nation—and the souls of individuals. As a result, true humility stands out.

Leadership researcher Jim Collins speaks of humility as a defining characteristic of "Level 5 leaders," the critical foundation to moving an enterprise from good to great:

> The most powerfully transformative executives possess a paradoxical mixture of personal humility and professional will. They are timid and ferocious. Shy and fearless. They are rare—and unstoppable.[1]

Timid and ferocious.

Shy and fearless.

As we become healthy, we realize we have nothing to gain by misrepresenting the truth; as we grow stronger in our souls, any subtle or enormous exaggerations naturally become less appealing, less tempting, less the norm. Instead, we lean heavily on the truth and avoid inflating our own importance or ego. It's a rare attitude that stands out in a world saturated with exaggeration and self-importance.

Humility is an imperative for living and leading from a healthy soul.

HUMBLE PIE

Many years ago, a pastor emailed me because he wanted to ask me something about a talk he'd heard me give. Of course, I was thrilled that he had reached out. Someone had finally seen the brilliance of what I was bringing! I arranged to take the call during a quiet hour when my children would be napping, and when the phone rang, my heart nearly skipped a beat.

I couldn't wait to bestow more wisdom.

He started off by thanking me for my time and then went on to say he was wondering if I could provide the source for one of the stories I had shared.

Gulp.

I told him the original source, he thanked me, said goodbye, and hung up.

That was it. Maybe a three-minute conversation.

Just when I thought I was finally breaking through, offering the kind of material that warranted follow-up calls (undoubtedly filled with appreciation), I was instead asked a question about my sources. What a humbling experience for me as a fledgling communicator!

If you're like me, you probably get the occasional opportunity to eat some proverbial humble pie. (I've had *many* slices since then!) I get it. We live in a world of fake-it-until-you-make-it. So often it seems, in our communities and cultures, that if others win, then we're losing, and that's the end of us. Every part of life becomes win or die, at all costs, even if the cost is our consciences. It can be hard to embrace humility in that kind of world.

Historian and Bible scholar John Dickson suggests that the virtue of humility simply did not exist until the person of Jesus Christ. In his book *Humilitas*, John points out that, based on the historical evidence, humility was seen as something to be avoided (think *humiliation*) until Jesus showed up on earth and began talking about it. Both *humility* and *humiliation* come from the root word *humus*, meaning "earth" or "ground," and neither sounds that appealing.

Being brought down to the level of the ground, either

voluntarily or by someone else, was not something to be pursued in a world that—then as still today—prioritizes winning. And yet Jesus endorsed it, taught us to practice it, and illustrated what it looks like. He was among the first to label humility a virtue, and the New Testament writers carried forward the refrain:

> Do nothing out of selfish ambition or vain conceit.
> Rather, in humility value others above yourselves,
> not looking to your own interests but each of you to
> the interests of the others.
>   In your relationships with one another, have the same
> mindset as Christ Jesus:
> Who, being in very nature God,
>   did not consider equality with God something to be used
>   to his own advantage;
> rather, he made himself nothing
>   by taking the very nature of a servant.
> **PHILIPPIANS 2:3-7**

> Humble yourselves, therefore, under God's mighty hand,
> that he may lift you up in due time.
> **1 PETER 5:6**

These Scriptures and others like them suggest that humility isn't a quality we simply do or do not possess but rather a choice we can make. Regularly.

But while humility is a choice, it does not seem to be one we can *easily* choose or even voluntarily submit to: Most often, humility seems to be something we gain through experience.

I certainly learned a lot about humility, about being brought low to the earth, during my illness. There's nothing like having your ability to care for yourself stripped away, to realize you can no longer provide for your own needs, to learn you are completely dependent on others. This dependency, this awareness of my weakness, was a starting point for my journey into humility, one I am still learning about and often failing to do well.

Being humbled is one path to humility. But humility doesn't have to be something we acquire only through difficult circumstances. I think the practice of humbling ourselves is something we can learn. Father Richard Rohr once said, "I have prayed for years for one good humiliation a day, and then I must watch my reaction to it."[2] In this way, *humility is a direction, a path, and a destination all at once*: We aim to live lives of humility, we choose to walk in it, and as we do, we increasingly find ourselves living in that place.

So how do we begin this journey?

DEVELOPING HUMILITY

To intend toward humility feels risky. We might fear loss of influence, loss of opportunity, loss of power, loss of control. But the good news is that deep soul health and the best kind of influence are actually available on the path of true humility, and we are all able to take steps to grow our capacity for humility. It might be a fairly narrow path, but the good ones usually are.

In his book *Hearing God*, Dallas Willard endorses a three-part maxim for developing humility:

> God will gladly give humility to us if, trusting and waiting on him to act, we refrain from *pretending* we are what we

know we are not, from *presuming* a favorable position for ourselves and from *pushing* or trying to override the will of others.[3]

Don't pretend. Don't presume. Don't push.

- *Pretend.* We often feel pressured to pretend in order to live up to or exceed the expectations of others. *What if they find out what my real online platform numbers are? Or my actual income? Or how many times I've been rejected?* We pretend to be something we're not to receive the kind of honor and respect we desire. The problem with pretending is that we are literally living a lie. We will never be able to keep up with the image we're projecting, and this sort of duplicitous living damages our souls. Don't pretend.

- *Presume.* When Jesus saw people jockeying for positions of honor at a table, he said, "When you are invited, take the lowest place, so that when your host comes, he will say to you, 'Friend, move up to a better place'" (Luke 14:10). Presuming we are owed a good seat at the table, that we somehow deserve more honor or recognition than someone else, shows an utter lack of humility; and in striving to be elevated, we will inevitably be cut down to size. Don't presume.

- *Push.* How many of us push for certain results assuming we know what is best for us and for others? When we choose not to push, we move instead toward surrender, letting go of the outcomes we expect and allowing God's ways to take precedence. When we entrust ourselves to the Good Shepherd, knowing that in God's good care all will be well, we're living within what Eugene Peterson called the unforced rhythms of grace. Don't push.

Don't pretend. Don't presume. Don't push. Instead, surrender to God's path, and act and speak with humility. This is the beginning of our journey to humility.

But there is more—the beginning of this journey also lies in a deep refusal to continue engaging in harmful past practices, including what Scot McKnight refers to as a "tolerance for false narratives."[4] Leaving falsehoods unaddressed is a surefire sign of a toxic space, whether it be in an office building or in a home. There is no need to lie in order to advance the work of God. Each time we do, a bit of our soul gets chipped away, and eventually we end up with very little of what is real. If we insist on continuing down this road, we will lose track of what is true and start believing our own lies.

There is one final vision of humility that I'd like to leave you with, one from South African pastor Andrew Murray:

> Humility is perfect quietness of heart. It is to expect nothing, to wonder at nothing that is done to me, to feel nothing done against me. It is to be at rest when nobody praises me, and when I am blamed or despised. It is to have a blessed home in the Lord, where I can go in and shut the door, and kneel to my Father in secret, and am at peace as in a deep sea of calmness, when all around and above is trouble.[5]

Humility is "perfect quietness of heart," not expecting that we will receive recognition or praise, but instead being at rest when we're not in the spotlight. At the heart of our humility is the knowledge that we don't receive our identity from recognition or honor given by men but rather find our identity when kneeling in front of our heavenly Father, in secret. I love that idea.

The practice of humility (or perhaps I should say the practice of seeking humility) is not only something we can achieve—it is also a path our souls need to walk if we are going to find soul health. We simply were not created to bear the burden of pride and recognition, of always being placed at the highest seat at the table. When we practice humility, intentionally seeking lower places, it is good for our souls.

And if humility is "perfect quietness of heart," then the next chapter's practice is one way of getting to that quiet place.

SOUL CARE REFLECTIONS

1. "Don't pretend. Don't presume. Don't push." Can you think of a situation in your life where you feel the need to pretend in order to make yourself, your family, your work, or your organization look better than it is? What do you fear would happen if you stopped pretending? What freedom might you find if you do stop?

2. Where might you have an elevated view of yourself? Is there an area where you are making presumptions based on that view? What might the impact of those presumptions be?

3. What circumstances in your life make you feel like you need to push hard in order to force an outcome? What fears lie

beneath that impulse to push? What are you concerned might happen if you stop pushing?

4. Reflect in your journal on what lies beneath your response to pretend, presume, or push. Write about what need or concern or motivating factor is causing you to do those things. How do these three areas reveal the well-being or dis-ease of your soul?

CALM AND QUIET

Practicing Silence

Silence first makes us pilgrims.
Secondly, silence guards the fire within.
Thirdly, silence teaches us how to speak.

HENRI NOUWEN, *The Way of the Heart*

That employee used up all their sick days this year—but were they really sick?

Why does that leader leave the office every day at five on the dot? Shouldn't they be working harder? Longer hours? They must not be very dedicated to their work.

How do they have time to get away, just the two of them? They must not care as much about their children.

That pastor went on a sabbatical. How does the church get by without him? He must not really care about his congregation as much as those pastors who never take time off.

How familiar are these questions?

Business people go into the office every day, often working long hours to the detriment of their families, their relationships, and their mental health. But this has been normalized to the point that, in some organizations, if a business person doesn't do this, they'll be fired, or at least viewed with suspicion.

Having children is a significant responsibility, one that should not be taken lightly. But society places incredible pressure on parents to be and do everything, and to make sure their kids are involved in every activity under the sun. When parents keep their kids out of certain activities, or when parents take a few days away, they can easily feel guilty, as though they aren't giving their children all they need or being the best parents they can be.

Pastors run themselves ragged serving people, because that is the greatest good, right—the ministry? Sharing the gospel? Somehow, overworking and not setting clear boundaries are seen as normal for being a pastor. And all too often this way of life leaves in its wake a pastor's own floundering marriage, addictions, or questionable moral choices. What would a congregation think if they saw their pastor stepping back, easing off the accelerator, or engaging in activities that were good for his soul even if it meant time away from the church?

Leaders regularly feel they must shoulder the weight of their entire organization. Stressed out, overworked leaders are so common, they're practically the norm. But all the while, they're unaware their own souls are dying. And secretly we wonder if leaders can be effective if they're working sensible hours and taking time for themselves and their families.

King David shouldered the weight of an entire nation and experienced the destructive side effects of an overextended soul: a family falling apart, broken relationships, addictions, questionable moral choices. And yet that was not the final verdict on his life. In a psalm ascribed to him, he writes:

> My heart is not proud, LORD,
>   my eyes are not haughty;
> I do not concern myself with great matters
>   or things too wonderful for me.
> *But I have calmed and quieted myself,*
>   *I am like a weaned child with its mother;*
>   *like a weaned child I am content.*
> Israel, put your hope in the LORD
>   both now and forevermore.

PSALM 131:1-3 (EMPHASIS ADDED)

Did you catch that middle verse?

"I have calmed and quieted myself . . . like a weaned child."

In the cacophony of life's demands and pressures, God invites us to still and quiet our souls. This invitation is entwined with another: "Be still, and know that I am God" (Psalm 46:10). We must know that God is God, but merely knowing is not enough: Our souls must learn how to rest in him truly.

When we let our soul rest in God's presence, we no longer come to him as an infant scrambling for sustenance or demanding his attention and action. Instead, we become like a content older child who just wants to be near for the sake of the relationship.

What does it look like to simply spend time with God, not because we approach with a list of things we want or need but because our hope is in God, and in God we find our contentment?

LISTEN TO YOUR SOUL

After my experience with vertigo forced me into a season of rest, my perspective about my value, my work, and my soul changed. In the summer of 1996, more than a year after that initial attack of paralyzing vertigo, I arranged to spend four hours at a Catholic retreat center in Dover, Massachusetts. In the stillness and quiet following my body's breakdown, I was beginning to hear the things my soul was craving. Getting away for a few hours at a time was one of them.

Listen to these gentle nudges from your soul.

As I drove the winding roads between Norwood and Dover toward the retreat center, my heart was in the right place, but my mind was still very much in control. How do I know this? Because I took ten books and my journal along with me to this four-hour retreat. I got settled into a peaceful library and then walked the beautiful trail on the grounds through meadows and along a bubbling brook. Even then, I still couldn't get my insides to slow down. My mind was spinning with all the worries and concerns of my life back in Norwood. Besides, I had a whole set of things I wanted to journal about, plus several books to read that undoubtedly held important answers for me in my soul-healing journey. I was ready to get to work.

After many fits and starts, trying to be still but finding stillness elusive, I finally experienced a place of peace for my soul toward the end of the afternoon, sitting on a bench in the sunshine. Of the four hours I spent there, fifteen minutes of stillness was all I could find.

And yet, even though that retreat felt a little bit like a failure, it mattered that I took the four hours—because the next time I went out there, finding a place of inner peace didn't take quite so long, and even less the next time, and so on.

Many of these soul-healing practices, I discovered, weren't things I could pick up in an instant and put on like an item of clothing. They would take time to work into. I wouldn't expect to run a marathon on my first day of exercise—that would be silly. In the same way, I'd have to build up some soul strength.

It didn't happen immediately, but each time I embraced the practices of silence or stillness or solitude or journaling, I learned to let go of my drivenness and release my need for productivity—and my soul would get stronger. As time went on, it became easier to enter into these practices. I could hear God's voice more clearly. When something difficult happened (or something exciting), I was able to navigate these experiences without huge swings in my mood or attitude.

Somehow stillness and silence, calm and quiet, are often the very things we need, the very things our souls crave, the very things that will bring healing to the most painful and broken parts of our lives.

SILENT PRAYER

Our souls long for health and the practices that will bring that health, but we have become adept at ignoring or suppressing that longing. That's why it's so important to engage in practices that elevate us above the fray of our lives, practices that help give us an objective distance and enable us to commune with God so that we can see our lives from his perspective. These practices disrupt our numbing routines and open us up so that we can see the Kingdom of God all around us.

In the months and years following my hospitalization, a mentor shared with me one of the most transformational practices she had ever engaged in: a wordless form of prayer that I have since called "silent prayer." The idea of silent prayer feels a bit illogical, since so much of how we think about prayer concerns words. But this form of prayer is actually about letting go of our words.

Silent prayer has become one of the most helpful and enduring practices in my life. But it can be challenging for those of us who are used to running through life at breakneck speed, either because of leadership responsibilities or community roles or when our homes are filled with the chatter and seemingly endless needs of little ones. When we're used to defining our lives by our productivity, it can be incredibly difficult to switch from the mindset that all meaningful accomplishments happen when we do something to the belief that sitting in silent prayer can perhaps be the most productive thing we can do in any given moment.

Silent prayer is a wordless way of resting in the presence of God with an attitude of openness, contrition, and longing. Too many of us are strangers with silence, strangers with sitting quietly and being with God. This must become a regular part of our lives if we want our souls to thrive. Silent prayer helps us discover that our souls know what we need even before our minds know something is missing or what options might fill the void.

The *how* of this form of prayer can vary, but my specific practice combines mindfulness principles with a focus on the Trinitarian nature of God. We're not simply opening up our minds to the universe; the words of Psalm 131:2 remind us we are entering into this form of prayer very much in God's presence— the Father, the Son, and the Spirit. As we rest our minds, stilling and quieting our souls in God's presence, we're inviting God, or offering a silent assent for him, to work in the innermost parts of our lives.

We get to simply rest in God's presence. Like a weaned, content child on their mother's lap.

Now, if you're like me, the moment you enter into silence, your mind is filled with a rush of thoughts: things you need to do, things you should be doing, people you're angry at or who are angry at you. Our minds, like water, become turbulent.

This is why, when we enter into this form of prayer, it's helpful to choose one word or phrase that embodies and anchors our desire for God—something like *peace* or *flourishing* or *Jesus* or *joy*. We stop long enough to notice that longing, perhaps writing down that word in a journal, and we allow it to tether us to the silence. When our minds get turbulent, the word can pull us back into quiet water, back to the reason for this time. We can stay there, resting in God's presence, trusting that at a level below words we're giving God access to the deepest parts of who we are, saying, *Have your way. Lead me.*

And then, seconds later, when new thoughts start coming, bombarding our minds with new worries, we can again use the word to bring us back to this central space of stillness.

Even merely entering into this space can change our breathing. It's a whole-body experience. I have found that silent prayer creates space in my day where I thought I didn't have space.

When silent prayer was first recommended to me as a practice, I was encouraged to do it twice a day for twenty minutes, and I laughed to myself because I didn't think I could do anything for twenty minutes, much less sit in silence! So I modified it to what I thought I could do: twenty minutes once a day, five days a week.

Even then, I didn't feel I had that kind of time. But my life was still in recovery from all that had happened, and I had a very strong sense that perhaps I didn't know how to run my life. Chaos, anxiety, an unhealthy relationship with work—all these had led me to a place where my body and mind had given out on me. One of the benefits of a breakdown is that it forces us to face our inability to control even the most vital, important things in our lives.

What I have discovered over the years is that silent prayer has opened me up to being present to God and to others without having an agenda—and it's opened me up to deep levels of healing. I encourage you: Don't be afraid of silence. Be willing to step into the quiet, and you will discover that God will meet you there.

BE NEAR

I had just returned from a long trip away, and we decided to go out to dinner as a family. I was so glad to be back in the presence of Jeff and the boys, and we enjoyed our time together that night. Then, at some point during the lull between the end of the meal and paying the bill, I noticed that our oldest son, Jeffrey, had been gradually inching his way closer to me until he'd reached the point where he was about as close to sitting on my lap as an eleven-year-old boy would ever be.

I could not remember the last time he had been this close. Long gone were the sleepy infant days, the snuggly toddler years, and the early–elementary school moments when he would still hold my hand. These were the days of nonstop action, the rough-and-tumble, mature, doesn't-need-his-mother preteen. When I realized what was happening, I remember wishing I could stop time. I knew the spell would be broken once we left to drive home—but oh, how I wished we could all stay just a bit longer. He wasn't asking for anything. He didn't "need" anything from me in that moment. He just wanted to be close. There were no words, no conversation, just the two of us sharing the same space and enjoying that sense of closeness.

To this day, that image invites me in toward God. If that's how much I as a human parent relish the nearness of my children, I can't help but wonder how much more that kind of closeness might delight and warm the heart of God. When I choose to move in close, not asking for or demanding anything but simply sharing the same space, I become aware of our closeness; I have chosen, out of all the other ways I could spend my time, to simply sit and be near to God.

What pleasure that must bring my heavenly Father!

When is the last time you calmed and quieted yourself, resting in the love and care of the almighty God of the universe, the one who created the heavens and the earth, the one who sees you completely, loves you fully, and with the loving gaze of heaven, knows absolutely everything about you? Dedicating time to this will do so much for your soul health, strengthening and healing and helping you become more sensitive to what God is saying to you in your everyday life. Practicing silence is a deeply restorative act, one that will prepare you for the journey ahead.

Open your soul in the presence of God and say, *Have your way.*

 ## SOUL CARE REFLECTIONS

1. When is the last time you sat in silence?

2. What comes to mind when you think of practicing silent prayer? Does this seem appealing or scary, fruitful or pointless?

3. Begin a daily practice of silent prayer. Perhaps start with five minutes a day, or if that seems like too much, try three minutes, and then, as the days and weeks progress, gradually add minutes.

4. Write in your journal about how the practice of silent prayer makes you feel, both during and afterward. How does silence impact your thinking, your attitude?

THE HARDEST TASK

Practicing Rest

Life from the Center is a life of
unhurried peace and power.

THOMAS R. KELLY, *A Testament of Devotion*

The assignment I gave to the leader seemed simple: set aside two hours for a solitude retreat. I'd developed a soul care plan for this leader, whom I know well and had worked with closely. The overall plan was to be a pathway uniquely designed to help them attend to their spiritual life, take care of their soul, and embrace the next stage of their journey.

Among the various reading selections and serving opportunities and practices and disciplines, this solitude retreat simply required *not* doing anything. The leader was to spend two hours alone with God, without their phone. Without their work.

That was it. That was the assignment. I wasn't asking them to spend an entire month away in a secluded spot; not a weekend in a remote cabin alone; not even half a day. Two hours.

Guess what?

Really hard work got done. Talks were written. Trips to global offices happened. Deals were negotiated. Budget projections were made, board presentations were created, staff were hired and fired. In other words, all hard deadlines were met and fires were put out. But in the span of two years, this leader, by their own admission, simply could not intentionally step away and stop being available. They couldn't stop being productive. They couldn't turn "off." It began to be a fun joke, and I believe as of this writing that they did finally go on this two-hour retreat, and many more such occasions have become habitual.

Turns out retreat is hard.

Pressing pause feels like it's beyond our reach.

Rest is nearly impossible for some of us.

But I have also come to believe that intentionally taking time away from our productivity to be alone with God, whether through solitude, retreat, Sabbath, or sabbatical, is actually one of the most important things we can do. In fact, we must do it. Without time away, we lose our bearing. We lose our being. We lose our humility. We lose our humanity.

And when we lose those things, it's just a matter of time until we lose everything. Until we lose our souls.

THE INVITATION TO RETREAT

What is the biggest challenge you face? Building a cohesive team? Communicating a clear vision? Developing a strategy to realize that vision? Is it securing funding? Recruiting volunteers and staff members?

Maybe you have small children and you're trying to find some space for yourself outside their many needs. Perhaps aging parents demand your time and attention as you help them navigate medical issues and transportation.

Or perhaps you're working through health challenges that have you feeling worn down and depleted.

Seriously. Stop for a moment and reflect: What's your biggest challenge right now?

Most of us, when faced with an important, urgent challenge, can sense the adrenaline start to build and will clear our schedules and forgo sleep if needed, doing whatever it takes to address and even conquer the looming challenge. We rise to the occasion, whether it be a crisis at work, a child's last-minute need, or a parent's health emergency.

Are you like this? You rise to the occasion. You do whatever it takes. Like Superman, you are "faster than a speeding bullet, more powerful than a locomotive, able to leap tall buildings in a single bound." When an employee or coworker quits or becomes sick, you step up and work harder to fill in the gaps. When your spouse is out of commission, you take over additional family responsibilities.

And you keep going.

At least, for the time being.

I celebrate this kind of perseverance, this kind of ownership. I recognize it in myself as well. Our capacities can accomplish great things, especially under the guidance and direction and empowerment of the Holy Spirit. We love quoting—and seeing—that "all things are possible."

But here's what I've also noticed in myself and others over the years: People who would not even flinch at spending thirty hours in transit to a speaking engagement, who are also negotiating major real estate transactions for their organizations and are also hiring key staff members (or caring for children at home while taking their parents to various medical appointments or responsible for developing visionary financial pro formas to present to their board next week while gearing up to bring a "fresh word" to that awaiting audience) all find it extremely difficult to do one thing—*retreat.*

We stay up all night, push past physical and emotional pain, ignore the pleas of friends and loved ones, and keep going, often "for the sake of the call," or so we think. Some of us openly vilify the very word, as if a halt in forward progress is a threat to our existence or an indictment of our character. But a bit of reflection usually reveals that our overdoing is often rooted in our egos, in not disappointing powerful people, in appeasing our fear of failure.

Before we get too frustrated with ourselves, though, let's remember: This resistance to rest and retreat is not a new or novel thing for the people of God. And to understand what's behind it, we don't have to look too far.

Throughout Scripture, we see dozens of invitations and admonitions, and even commandments, to live and lead out of a place of rest: God introduces, almost immediately, a pattern of Sabbath and gives the Israelites the Year of Jubilee; Jesus further shows us this through his habits of solitude, stillness, and prayer. These are things the Lord has created, modeled, and invited us into that reinforce rhythms of rest and retreat.

Yet rest and retreat, while having many gifts to give, also requires something of us: trust. That's what makes it so hard. If we are going to truly rest and retreat, we have to have a deep and

THE HARDEST TASK

abiding sense of trust that God will sustain us and all the things we are involved in, even as we step away.

One of my favorite passages from all of Scripture, Isaiah 30:15, reads like this:

> This is what the Sovereign Lord, the Holy One of Israel, says:

> "In repentance and rest is your salvation,
>   in quietness and trust is your strength,
>   but you would have none of it."

Can you hear the ache in God's voice saying, "but you would have none of it"? God offered himself as his people's protection and strength, but they went out and secured what they thought would be sources of provision and security instead: faster horses so they could flee from their oppressors, alliances with powerful neighboring nations, anything this world could offer to ensure their well-being.

And yes, we do the same today, working harder and harder in order to "guarantee" our well-being, our financial stability, our children's futures, and any number of things we don't actually have control over.

But God aches over you and me when we choose to go elsewhere to ensure our well-being. He wants nothing more than for us to completely trust him in regard to our provision, our peace, and our safety.

Even today, he says to us: "In repentance and rest is your salvation."

Can you hear God's longing to be our provider, our protector, our source? God's sadness over knowing what and who we become when we choose otherwise?

God spoke about rest and retreat through his prophets in the Old Testament, but he modeled it for us in the person of Jesus. There's a story in Mark 1 that comes right on the heels of a successful ministry event. These days we might even refer to it as a revival. Jesus was preaching and healing people and drawing larger and larger crowds.

What would we do in that kind of a situation?

Would we keep working, doing more and more? *Look at all the advancement being made for the Kingdom! We wouldn't want to jeopardize that!*

Would we call in for more disciples? *Now is the time! We have to strike while the iron is hot!*

Or would we retreat and rest?

Somehow, in the midst of that budding revival, that is what Jesus does:

> Very early in the morning, while it was still dark, Jesus
> got up, left the house and went off to a solitary place,
> where he prayed. Simon and his companions went to
> look for him, and when they found him, they exclaimed:
> "Everyone is looking for you!"
> **MARK 1:35-37**

Jesus retreated to be with God. He left the crowds behind. And "irresponsibly" enough, he didn't even tell his followers where he was going! What if they would have needed him for something? What if something had gone horribly wrong? What if someone in a position of power had wanted to talk with him, to support them, to help the cause? What if someone had needed healing or demon-possessed people had approached?

His followers' reaction sounds familiar to me: *Jesus, where did you go? There are things to be done, people to be healed, sermons to be preached!*

Everyone is looking for you!

When we consider our current models of ministry and ways of operating, rest and retreat almost sound silly. To walk away just when things are beginning to take off seems foolish, even irresponsible. After all, we are here to help people find eternal life.

Whatever the cost.

Whatever the cost?

If rest and retreat are essential, they might also sometimes appear ill-timed. Inappropriate or irresponsible even.

But if God in human form chose to rest and retreat, how much more do we need to do the same?

HOW TO RETREAT

God commanded us to rest, and Jesus showed us how it's done. Even the secular world around us is beginning to recognize how integral rest and retreat are to human flourishing. A recent Forbes article[1] lists five benefits that occur when you ensure you are receiving adequate rest:

- *Physical healing.* The human body flourishes in short bursts of activity, so taking a break, even for a few minutes, can refresh us throughout the day. "Adequate rest helps your body activate its inner healing cascade and return to a state of homeostasis."[2] In other words, resting helps your body make repairs and recover from the hard work you're doing.

- *Stress reduction.* When you're stressed, you experience a fight-or-flight response, something that may make you feel more productive, at least in the short term. But our bodies were not made to remain in that state. "Resting activates the parasympathetic nervous system—the opposite of the . . . flight-or-fight response."[3] Resting can lower your heart rate and blood pressure, bring your digestive function back to a normal pace, and decrease hormone levels that cause stress.

- *Boosted creativity.* Resting allows you time to refill your reserves, reflect, and break through creative walls. Open-ended problems become more easily solved because your brain has the space to act spontaneously.

- *Improved productivity.* Your brain is like most of your other muscles—it is less functional when it's fatigued. Rest sharpens your thinking.

- *Enhanced decision-making.* Working for too long without resting or a retreat leads to a lower ability to concentrate and depreciated emotional capacity.

These benefits only expand when we engage in more intentional, extended times of rest, such as retreats or even sabbaticals. Several friends of mine have recently stepped away from their senior leadership responsibilities for a summer in order to take a sabbatical, some for as little as a month, others for three or more months. What a wise and strategic thing to do! A sabbatical, however, is not just an extended vacation. There is so much more to glean from this gift than simply time away: a broader perspective on life; a clearer connection with God, free of the normal distractions and responsibilities; and the opportunity to see, with God's help, where and how our lives are connecting with the Kingdom of God.

And lest you think that sabbaticals are only possible in Christian ministry, the concept has actually begun to move into the mainstream. *Harvard Business Review* notes,

> While the type (paid versus unpaid), length (weeks versus months), and other sabbatical details vary, research suggests that the upward trend in sabbaticals is due to two primary factors. Sabbaticals and extended vacation time are not just good for employees to rest and recharge—they benefit the organization by stress-testing the organizational chart and providing interim roles to allow aspiring employees to take on more leadership.[4]

Retreats and sabbaticals allow you to get to a space where the noise floor of your life can actually drop. Times of real, extended rest aren't for binge-watching or socializing with friends or going for long runs. Those things have their place, but not as part of solitude and retreat. There, your mind can become still, focused on being with God, resting in God, and connecting with God.

So what could intentional times of retreat look like for you?

Start with an honest look at your calendar. Is it maxed out? Is there margin for rest? Most people end up being quite surprised at how easy it is to make adjustments ahead of time. How you spend your time, and with whom, is one of the biggest factors in your overall rule of life. Be sure to incorporate rest and retreat and silence and solitude into that plan.

Where and when will you pause, disconnect from your productivity and sense of being "on," and connect with God? For some, this looks like waking early in the morning, before the rest of the house, to light a candle and silently rest in God's presence as they begin a new day. For others, it's essential to go elsewhere physically—to a nearby comfortable hotel lobby, or a public library, or a park, or even a coffee shop. Whatever spot it is, getting away from the familiar and seemingly endless responsibilities that home or the office represent is essential. For an extended time of sabbatical, choosing a retreat center or other "away from the everyday" overnight accommodations allows you to maximize this unique gift of extended time set apart for reflection, rest, and a neurological reset.

Wherever you land, for however long you have, allow your mind, your body, your soul to truly sink into the experience. Notice what feels challenging, and rather than try to change any particular reaction that you notice, simply talk with God about whatever thoughts and feelings come up for you during this time. Invite God to speak to you quite personally about what you are experiencing.

If the concept of personal retreat is unfamiliar and foreign, there will be a learning curve. Stepping away will be hard, and all your muscle memory, everything in you, will be screaming and shouting loudly for you to remain productive, telling you that you have no value apart from what you do or accomplish or own.

Here are a few things that have helped me:

- *Enter each new day from a place of grounded peace.* Somewhere along the way, I realized that I had a pattern of waking up to the screaming demands of each day, whether they were young children or pressing deadlines, and then spending the rest of each day breathlessly reacting to whatever came my way. My mind and body were always on alert, scanning for the next demand or disaster. As it turns out, that's not a great way to show up in the world!

For many years now, I have instead found ways to begin each day on my own terms, at peace, in quiet, and with God. Pausing long enough to truly center, listen, breathe, reflect, and embrace gratitude.

Whether you only have five minutes or much more time, make sure you deliberately pause at the beginning of each new day. Maybe light that candle. Maybe wake up thirty minutes earlier. Maybe sit in silent prayer or reflect in the pages of a journal. Whatever it is, even taking five minutes to breathe deeply, creates an opportunity to reconnect with God's presence all around you. Receiving the new day with gratitude and expectation will allow you to move into it with an entirely different energy.

• *Schedule time away for solitude, and then invite others into your time . . . so you're accountable to do it!* Group solitude may seem like an oxymoron, but it really has some staying power. For the past several years, I have been hosting what I call a semi-silent retreat on a monthly basis for this very reason. We incorporate time for silence and for interaction. A fun virtual community is growing up around it, but everyone knows I started these in part for selfish reasons—to make sure I actually took a few hours each month for a time of personal solitude.

• *Commit to a twenty-four-hour floating Sabbath.* Many of us in various professions do not necessarily get a weekend day off. I get it. You might not get Sundays off. Or Saturdays. Or Mondays, Wednesdays, or Fridays. Maybe you're on the road a lot, and your schedule changes each week. Maybe you do generally have weekends free from office-hour expectations, but your work always seems to require weekend time simply to maintain progress. Or maybe your work is your home environment, which never, ever stops.

What I have discovered is this: The principle behind the Sabbath, the resting in God, the not being "on," is vital, and so is the expanded time frame of twenty-four hours where you are not "on"—not advancing a particular agenda, not striving for the next horizon. While that principle endures, what fluctuates is the time each week I dedicate to being "off." I find it helpful to draw an imaginary line in my schedule . . . and commit to not pushing forward for the next twenty-four hours. Sometimes it's Friday at 3:00 p.m.; sometimes it's Sunday at noon. But usually between Friday and Monday, I can carve out those sacred twenty-four Sabbath hours to be "off."

If your schedule can accommodate the Sabbath being the same time frame each week, I do think that would be an even more useful practice for your body and soul. But if your schedule does not permit that level of routine, please at least make sure you can carve out those twenty-four consecutive hours to be "off." Yes, you're still with family and friends; yes, you're out for a walk or reading a great book, but you're not "on." You're not pushing forward. You're able to rest. Trust. Enjoy God and others. Recreate and relax. Replenish and restore. Remember and rest.

If retreat is already a common practice for you—and I hope perhaps it already is—please begin to take some others along with you on this journey. As Eli did for young Samuel, help someone else begin to discern the voice of God in their own life. Help those behind you, in age or life stage, form patterns of rest and retreat early on in their lives. Model this for your children.

What I have noticed as I embrace rest and retreat on a weekly and monthly basis is this: I remain clear on who is God and who is not. I am refreshed in my spirit. My soul gets restored. I reanchor my doing into God's being and my own being.[5]

Retreat and rest can't be something we only do when we have nothing else to do. Retreat and rest are actually a strategic priority.

So pull out your calendar, make a few changes if necessary, find several hours—even a half day if possible—to do a mini retreat monthly. Give it a try for a few months, and then evaluate.

Set an earlier alarm each morning, and even a timer if it helps guard your quiet start to the day.

Whichever path you choose, recognize that none will be easy.

But you didn't sign up for easy; you want a flourishing life. And rest is a *key* ingredient.

Do the hard thing.

SOUL CARE REFLECTIONS

1. What does your actual calendar suggest about the value you currently place on rest, retreat, and solitude? Do you like what you see?

2. When is the last time you felt deeply rested? What were you doing, or not doing, at that time?

3. Carve out a twenty-four-hour Sabbath this week. Make note in a journal or on your calendar what time it starts and ends. Start paying attention to your capacity for rest.

4. Arrange for a three-hour retreat sometime in the next month, and see if you can enlist a buddy to share the experience! Be sure to notice what resistance comes up for you, and reflect on it in a journal.

SOUL FLOURISHING

The God of Scenario Q

Trust God that you are exactly
where you are meant to be.

ST. TERESA OF AVILA

Back in 1996 and 1997, the years following my hospitalization
and eventual diagnosis of this debilitating vertigo, I began meeting
with a small group of women. We had all, in one way or another,
come to the end of our ropes, finding ourselves quite willing to—
as the beginning of the Twelve Steps directs—admit "we were powerless," make "a decision to turn our will and our lives over to the
care of God," admit to God and each other the "exact nature of
our wrongs," and be ready for God to "remove all these defects of
character."[1] In short, we were tired of all the posturing and mask
wearing that was going on out there, and we were ready to be
vulnerable with one another.

As we entered into these spaces of prayerfulness, ready to

surrender to how God might intervene in our lives, we began to see a pattern.

We started referring to it as Scenario Q.

Often, when we get together with others and pray for things going on in our lives, we'll pray for Scenario A. That's the thing we really want to happen. So maybe if someone in the group wanted a new job, we'd pray that she'd get this certain job she really wanted. That would be Scenario A.

Scenario B would be having to settle for a job she really didn't want but had to take because she needed a job, so that was an option too. But Scenario A is still what we prayed for, and we really didn't want Scenario B to happen.

All the while, Scenario C was lurking, which would probably be something in between the dream job and the job of necessity, something that checked a few of the boxes and wasn't soul killing. And at the end of the day, most of us kind of think that Scenario C is what happens in the end, right? Because, normally, the dream thing doesn't come true, but the worst doesn't often happen either, so we all assume Scenario C will take place.

We've become used to living our lives in Scenario C.

But this is where Scenario Q comes in.

What we began to see and experience in our group of women was this: Whatever we were praying about, whether marriage difficulties or a new job or stuff going on with our kids, we were being honest about what we wanted and didn't want, honest about our tendency to settle. And then, before any of the scenarios we imagined would play out, Scenario Q would unfold.

Scenario Q was the thing that happened that we never could have imagined or envisioned. We saw a problem or a life situation and thought we could see all the different ways this thing was going to play out: Scenario A, Scenario B, or Scenario C. But then Scenario Q would come into being, something completely off our radar, utterly outside what we had hoped for.

Again and again this would happen. And when it would happen, we'd be wholly caught off guard. But what we started to realize, and what was so beautiful about Scenario Q, is that even when we were thinking about and praying for A, B, and C, what our specific scenarios tended not to capture was a deeper desire. Each and every time, Scenario Q both surfaced and fulfilled that foundational desire.

For me, it can look like this: Scenario A is a particular job I really want, or a certain living situation. Perhaps it's a friendship I really desire to have or the outcome of a project at work. It's the ideal future for everything I'm currently in the middle of. Then, Scenario B is the thing I really *don't* want in the above situations. Perhaps it's that I end up being stuck at the job I have or in a particular painful living situation. The person I wanted to be friends with ignores my overtures. The project fails. Publicly. So I earnestly pray to God for the seen outcomes I imagine in Scenario A, and I beg God to be spared from Scenario B. All the while, I'm mentally preparing myself for some compromise position that I somehow think is likely or possible.

I brace myself for Scenario C, which in this case might represent a slight adjustment in my role at work, a slightly favorable shift in my living situation, a socially engaged but not spiritually satisfying friendship, or moderate success in the project I'm working on.

Underneath all these scenarios, both imagined and eventual, is longing. In those specific situations, I longed for the work I did to bring value and meaning. I longed for our young family to have what it needed in this next season to support our growth. I longed for deep and meaningful friendships. I longed for the future of a massive global vision called Soul Care.

But Scenario Q showed up to meet that longing with something I simply never could have foreseen: a complete relocation to a new city, a wildly different home base for our family, friendships that endure the distance and others that deepen with fresh proximity, complete abandonment of the projects I had been working so hard to develop.

When those sorts of things happen, we can't see them coming. They're so far outside what we think is within the realm of possibility. By definition, Scenario Q is impossible to predict, impossible to forecast.

But Scenario Q isn't a given. If we can't open ourselves up to new things, if we stay so locked into our preconceived ideas of what should be, we can miss what God actually is up to. Some people want following God to be a way of life that guarantees all our prayers are getting answered exactly as we request. Scenario Q invites us to receive a better way than anything we could imagine, to recognize that God may be preparing us to meet him in deeper realities than we even understood we needed. Remember the hinge point, where the invisible Kingdom comes into contact with our tangible lives? That's where Scenario Q exists. It's when something happening in the unseen breaks into the seen, and we have a resolution, at least for a season.

Soul care is not an invitation into a list of new things you can do. It is not about engaging in new practices simply to be able to say you do them. It is not simplicity for the sake of simplicity, or solitude for the sake of alone time, or silent prayer for the sake of silent prayer.

Soul care gets you ready for Scenario Q before you even know it could be an option.

Soul care is a way of life that allows you to develop the heart, mind, and spirit to become a person of the Kingdom, an active participant with God in the here and now.

There's nothing wrong with desiring Scenario A. God specifically invites us to ask, seek, and knock. But when your soul is healthy, you're wearing knee holes into the carpet, desperately giving yourself over to God, seeking his voice on Scenario A but also open to whatever he wants to do. You've realized that you don't know the first thing about what's best for you. You know you can perhaps imagine what's best or come up with something that seems like an improvement, but you live in the greater reality: that God may want to do something you never could have hoped for or even imagined.

The fruit of this kind of life is that you become aware of, and open to, a Scenario Q if it starts to unfold. You can notice God working, and you can rest in trust when you're waiting for him to move. You're free to live in the ache and the beauty of Isaiah 43:16-19:

> This is what the LORD says—
>> he who made a way through the sea,
>> a path through the mighty waters,
> who drew out the chariots and horses,
>> the army and reinforcements together,
> and they lay there, never to rise again,
>> extinguished, snuffed out like a wick:
> "Forget the former things;
>> do not dwell on the past.

See, I am doing a new thing!
Now it springs up; do you not perceive it?
I am making a way in the wilderness
and streams in the wasteland."

God is doing a new thing, something we cannot even perceive. When we build in a capacity to be still, to practice silent prayer, to be open and surrendered to God bringing new things into our lives, we break out of our preconceived ideas about what the range of possibilities might be.

We stop getting preoccupied with Scenarios A, B, and C.

We know that God is behind the scenes, preparing Scenario Q.

LIVING FROM A HEALTHY SOUL

The real-life implications of becoming people who trust for Scenario Q are this: Two people may experience similar circumstances and respond in completely different ways, depending on the health of their souls.

Even if both of them are Christians.

Let's say there are two women: Mandi and Ella.

Mandi's time is taken up quite a bit with caring for her aging parents—not that either of them are seriously ill, but they require help around the house, occasional transportation to doctors' appointments, and general support. Mandi also has two children, one in college and one in high school. Because of college tuition, Mandi has taken on a part-time job, and she's also heavily involved in the PTA at her younger child's high school. There are plenty of events to attend.

Mandi and her husband have an average relationship. They get along, rarely fight, and keep the peace, but they're both so busy that they hardly see each other or have time to go out together. They are both hanging on for a time in life when the pace is more manageable.

Mandi has friends but, again, very little time to catch up with them. She used to go to a therapist when she was in her thirties, but she no longer does that. She tries to read her Bible when she can, but since the pandemic, she and her husband have fallen out of the habit of going to church every week. They still try to get there at least once or twice a month.

When Mandi does have any free time—usually at night when she can't fall asleep—she'll turn on the TV to watch Netflix while scrolling through Facebook on her phone. Before she knows it, it's well after midnight and her husband is already asleep, so she creeps to bed and tries to climb in without waking him.

When it comes to practices that care for her soul, Mandi thinks they sound nice, even appealing; but who has time for that?

Sound familiar?

Meanwhile, Ella experiences many of the same circumstances—she's bookended by her parents and older teens, all of whom need her support, encouragement, and attention. She has a part-time job and is involved in her younger child's school. She and her husband have a good relationship. She's very busy.

In fact, the only real difference between Mandi and Ella is that for two or three years now, Ella has been taking care of her soul in various ways. When she told her husband how much she enjoys walking in the morning, he took over seeing their youngest out the door to high school so Ella could hit the trails behind their house. Ella also practices silent prayer most days. She makes a deliberate choice to look for opportunities where God might be inviting her

to work together with him in small ways in her neighborhood—
saying hi to her elderly neighbor or making cookies during the
holidays for some of the families around them.

Already, I think you can sense a difference between Mandi's
life and Ella's life. Their ordinary, day-to-day existence is substan-
tially different, simply because of the practices that Ella has introduced into her life. Ella's days feel sustainable, even the busy ones,
because she is constantly reconnecting with her center, journaling
about issues she has, and reaching out to her friends or counselor
when something begins to feel off. When she encounters a setback
or disappointment, she has learned to remain connected to God,
receive her value and identity and strength and direction from that
real-time connection, and trust that he is working in ways that will
meet her needs more deeply than she knows. This is how it looks
to live with Scenario Q in mind.

Mandi, meanwhile, lives a chaotic schedule. She is operating at
seven thousand RPMs, and that's just when life is normal. Mandi
thinks she knows the best outcome in almost every situation
(Scenario A), and she feels disappointment, anxiety, and sometimes even despair when things don't work out the way she had
hoped. She's constantly putting out fires, and she frequently feels
that she's all alone, not good enough, too busy, and wishing life
wasn't the way it was.

What happens when something devastating enters the equation?

Mandi finds out that one of her children has been experimenting with drugs, and her self-worth as a parent plummets.
She wonders how she could have missed this and beats herself up
constantly for not recognizing the signs. In order to support her
daughter, she quits work and spends most of her days worrying
nonstop about whether her daughter is making better choices.

Finally, things hit rock bottom: Mandi's father is the one who is ill, but it's her mother who dies unexpectedly. This throws her into a complete tailspin.

The grief is overwhelming, and she has no one to turn to, no friends to talk about it with, and no foundational spiritual practices to help keep her anchored during this incredibly difficult storm. She begins engaging in addictive behaviors in order to numb the pain she's feeling and to cloud the worry that overwhelms her.

Scenario B happened in her life—her child's addiction, her parent's passing. The outcomes she had hoped would never take place. She feels lost, unmoored.

Where Mandi's life goes from here is a complete unknown. Maybe she's able to pull up out of her despair on her own, maybe she can talk herself out of this new addiction, maybe she can repair her now-nonexistent relationship with her husband. The truth is that without having done any positive spiritual formation work, what Mandi's life will look like in a few short months or years is completely up for grabs. Hopefully someone will become her guide, as many were for me.

How does someone like Ella respond to similar circumstances?

In my experience, the spiritual formation Ella was involved in will bring her through the desolation. When she discovers her child has been experimenting with drugs, she doesn't immediately plunge into the depths of despair. Instead, she turns to her journal, where she can work through the ways this threatens to tear down her own self-worth. She calls her spiritual director or therapist and immediately schedules time with them to work through these issues. And with their help, along with the introspection she's been doing in her journal, she can make a plan to move forward—all while trusting that God loves her child more fiercely than she ever can, and that he can and will move in ways she doesn't expect. She realizes—no, she believes—that all these things are leading to an end that she could never imagine, and she trusts that in this Scenario Q she will grow closer to God and be a hinge-point person, bringing the Kingdom into her tangible life.

Like Mandi, she also quits her part-time job, but because she's spending time in silent prayer, and because she knows the importance of rest as a weapon, she naps when she's tired and doesn't allow guilt to motivate her.

When her mother dies, she's devastated, but she doesn't try to numb her pain with pills or alcohol or busyness or shopping or television. She simply gives herself time and space to sit in the desolation and experience the grief that has come. She is alert to what is now possible in the changing landscape of her life. She is expectant of the new thing God will be doing while being fully present to the grief of what has been lost. She's trusting for Scenario Q.

Months down the road, Ella's relationships with her husband and children are actually stronger than when the devastation first hit. She feels closer to God because of how these foundational spiritual practices helped her not only work through the circumstances but also see where and how God was working and calling her to work together with him.

Again, simply doing the practices doesn't make a difference. The difference comes because of how those things train our souls to attend to God—to operate day in and day out with God. If we have time to set aside for silence, then that's wonderful; but the more we practice silence, the more easily we can attend to God even when we're in the car or the grocery line or on a work Zoom call. We can experience the awareness of, and responsiveness to, God's presence wherever we are, and we begin to participate with

God in all sorts of ways. Then, as we trust God's guidance and heart for us, we find steady ground in both the good and the hard, for our souls are truly well.

THE HARD AND THE GOOD

Caring for your soul doesn't mean hard or terrible things won't happen to you. Caring for your soul doesn't exempt you from making bad decisions or suffering losses or making mistakes. But the reality of the Kingdom of Heaven is that God is enough to sustain you, and he'll keep guiding you in all circumstances. When your soul is healthy, you discover a lightness of being, an awareness that God is still on the move, whether in the midst of destruction or good news, heartache or joy.

The year of the Marshall Fire was the most disruptive year of my life since my vertigo in 1995. My rhythms were off, my sense of place was completely gone; I was showering in the local gym, and we were living in a home rented through Airbnb. I got increasingly agitated using someone else's towels and sleeping on someone else's sheets, having my morning coffee and silence on someone else's couch, living with the underlying disruption of selling a house, moving everything into storage, keeping up with my travel and work commitments, and walking with our community as we suffered this incredible loss together.

I just wanted to be home. In my own home. But that was not going to happen anytime soon.

We experienced so much grace in that situation, especially in the beginning, but after a few months, I grew tired of living out of our luggage and storage units. There was so much to do, so much beyond what we do in normal life. Plus we were rebuilding what had been destroyed on our property, planting over a hundred trees, drilling unsuccessfully for water. The list goes on and on.

At the same time, there were moments and days that were so sweet and beautiful. We got to spend the summer in an RV, and there are few things more glorious than waking up in the high desert along the Rocky Mountains, making coffee in the camper, and then stepping outside to have morning silence on a small stone patio as the sunrise spills over Eldorado Canyon and Boulder's Flatirons.

That was also the year we experienced both intense emotions and sweet kindness as we finally got to gather in upstate New York with our entire family and many childhood friends to honor and celebrate my dad's life. He had passed away in 2020, and because one of my five brothers and his family live in New Zealand, we hadn't yet been able to gather due to COVID travel restrictions. While getting together with everyone and celebrating Dad's incredible life and legacy was joy filled and beautiful, it was also intense and achy. Grief had been delayed, arrived in waves, and is ongoing.

That season brought so many transitions, many of them welcomed and even needed. We celebrated our son's engagement. We relocated yet again to a beautiful home in a nearby community as the burned-out neighborhoods began the long process of rebuilding. And I felt carried along by God's favor and grace the whole time. The land had been cleared in my life. I was just trying to pay attention so that I could see the new things appearing.

Few situations in my life during those days worked out to my imagined Scenarios A, B, or C. And yet I was able to experience so many Scenario Qs that were beautiful, tailored perfectly for our life at the time, reminding me of the unseen Kingdom where God is always at work.

This is the beauty of soul care. In many ways, what happened with the fire mirrored what had happened in Boston twenty-five years earlier—except that this time I didn't fall apart. The year of the fire was extremely hard and disruptive, emotionally draining and exhausting. But this time around I was able to stay deeply connected to God in the midst of the hard, which opened me up to the good—and made it possible for me to be at peace.

THE SOUL AT PEACE

Growing up in the Catholic church, I always looked forward to the point in each Mass when the priest would invite us to "pass the peace." We would turn to strangers, family members, and friends and say, "Peace be with you."

But peace can be quite elusive, both interpersonally and even internally. We need peace now more than ever, and the availability of what many call "inner peace" is a rare and noticeable trait. I don't think there's ever been a time when we've needed to pass—transmit—peace more than we do right now. To each other, to strangers, and sometimes even to ourselves.

These days, I find myself noticing the longing for peace, not just in my circumstances and relationships but in my very body. I have learned to pay attention to when my body is holding tension—when my forehead is tight, my neck or shoulders frozen. My brain may know that it is well with my soul, but no one has told the shoulders inching their way toward my ears.

One time, driving between appointments, I realized my body was carrying a ton of stress. My mind had reviewed the circumstances and had recommitted to trusting God, but apparently my shoulders had not yet clued in. They were convinced that this situation was a threat, warranting anxiety.

It seems funny now, but I remember thinking I needed to convince my deltoids and trapezius that all would be well. I began to say out loud to my own body, "Peace be with you!" Sometimes we need to pass the peace to ourselves: to remind ourselves what is true and what God offers.

Interestingly, the only time we hear Jesus say "Peace be with you" is following the Resurrection, the ultimate Scenario Q. The Temple curtain is torn, there's been an earthquake, people long dead have been raised. Jesus, scars still visible, is alive. A dead man is walking, talking, relating, eating—but no longer bound by the constraints of the physical world.

No one saw Scenario Q coming except for Jesus, who predicted both his death and resurrection multiple times. And isn't that always how it works? God is never, ever, ever surprised when the unseen breaks forth into the seen.

And after his resurrection, God in the flesh carried a new greeting to the disciples who were huddled together in fear for their lives: *Peace be with you.*

> On the evening of that first day of the week, when the disciples were together, with the doors locked for fear of the Jewish leaders, Jesus came and stood among them and said, "*Peace be with you!*" After he said this, he showed them his hands and side. The disciples were overjoyed when they saw the Lord.
>
> Again Jesus said, "*Peace be with you!* As the Father has sent me, I am sending you." And with that he breathed on them and said, "Receive the Holy Spirit. If you forgive

anyone's sins, their sins are forgiven; if you do not forgive
them, they are not forgiven."

Now Thomas (also known as Didymus), one of the
Twelve, was not with the disciples when Jesus came. So
the other disciples told him, "We have seen the Lord!"

But he said to them, "Unless I see the nail marks in
his hands and put my finger where the nails were, and
put my hand into his side, I will not believe."

A week later his disciples were in the house again, and
Thomas was with them. Though the doors were locked,
Jesus came and stood among them and said, "Peace be
with you!" Then he said to Thomas, "Put your finger here;
see my hands. Reach out your hand and put it into my
side. Stop doubting and believe."

JOHN 20:19-27 (EMPHASIS ADDED)

So how does Jesus' greeting relate to the state of our souls?

The ancient concept of peace (*shalom* in Hebrew; *eirēnē* in
Greek) is much more comprehensive than merely a lack of inter-
personal conflict. Theologian Cornelius Plantinga explains the
biblical imagination around shalom this way:

In the Bible, shalom means *universal flourishing, wholeness,
and delight*—a rich state of affairs in which natural needs
are satisfied and natural gifts fruitfully employed, a state
of affairs that inspires joyful wonder as its Creator and
Savior opens doors and welcomes the creatures in whom
he delights. Shalom, in other words, is the way things
ought to be.[2]

When things are the way they ought to be within our souls, we experience *inner peace*. Even when surrounding circumstances are dire and grim, our souls can be well because Jesus moves through the walls of our self-protection and offers us his kind of peace.

The promise of shalom in daily life is that we can and will experience inner peace no matter what. This is the sure testimony of life under the care of our Good Shepherd, life anchored to the unseen.

When our souls are well, when peace is our way of life, our flourishing is not only for ourselves but becomes part of the gospel—the Good News—we knowingly or unknowingly convey to everyone around us. When we walk and move and contend and suffer and sacrifice and lead and follow with actual inner peace, everyone can sense it. There's peace in the way you talk to and treat the stressed checkout attendant at the grocery store. There's peace when things go wrong and you don't get caught up in it. There's peace when you find yourself in a new context or conversation and you are unruffled and secure.

For a world of souls on fire, of people feeling exhausted and empty and alone, the peace of a healthy soul speaks of a life everyone is dying to experience.

A WAY OF LIFE

In the middle of the crisis is a profoundly difficult time to learn the practices that care for our souls. It's nearly impossible to learn how to settle in solitude or how to be like a weaned child on their parent's lap when the fire alarms are all going off, when the relationship is falling apart, or when the career has disintegrated. There's space during those difficult times to *do* the practice, but rarely enough time or space to *learn* the practice.

If taking care of my soul hadn't become a way of life for me prior to 2022, I very well could have entered another free fall, hitting rock bottom in my mind, body, and soul. The natural thing that happens in a time of desperation, when you don't already have soul care practices in place, is for the portions of the brain with a primary role in processing emotional responses like fear or anxiety to take over. We end up running around with our hair on fire, scrambling for our sense of worth and our reason for existence. To respond differently than that is certainly possible, but it's a learned posture.

Because soul care had become my way of life long before the tumult of that year, I was equipped to enter the Garden of Desolation. I was able to keep space for God and be on the lookout for Scenario Q. My husband, Jeff, and I made shrewd decisions and bold moves, even in the middle of one of the toughest years of our life together. We sold our house, moved into an RV, bought a house, and formed a team around the mission of Soul Care. We began offering soul care experiences on the land and even created an eight-week journey called SOS (Strengthening Our Souls).

Even when the fear-and-anxiety part of my brain got loud, I had developed practices that helped me remain in stillness. When I entered into appointments with my spiritual director, I wasn't consumed with concerns about what she thought of me or whether I was saying the right things in the right ways. One of the times I spoke with her on the phone, I was sitting in a folding chair out in the middle of a field adjacent to an event somewhere in Kansas City because it was the only time we could actually talk. I was taking notes as quickly as I could, processing some emotions that my dad's celebration of life service had triggered, working through everything having to do with the fires, thinking through family relationships. The sun scorched down on me, but you can bet I kept the appointment for that phone call, because I knew I needed help. And her help helped.

The practice of soul care helps me notice the state of my soul and engage with God anywhere, whether in a field or in a hotel room or at the ranch with beautiful views or inside my own car in traffic. I can practice silent prayer in my office or my basement, on the deck or on a hike. These rhythms have been so worn into my soul that the practice is welcome regardless of my physical circumstances.

Hear me on this: I'm not saying that soul care is a magic bullet for every struggle you have in life. But soul care does create within us the resiliency and peace to weather the storms.

I believe there is a wave of healing coming in these next few years. Healing that will come as millions of people courageously do what it takes to arrange their lives around the well-being of their souls. People who can endure suffering, who can allow their pain to become metabolized into wisdom. People who can truly care for those around them and selflessly remain at the often uncomfortable hinge point between the seen and the unseen, contending for what is good and right and just and true and generative in our world.

Those people will be marked by inner peace. They'll have natural capacities for kindness. They'll be radiant with unwavering hope. Their humility will be striking, even compelling. People marked by soul health will illustrate for all to see what a human soul alive to God is really like. There is no greater apologetic.

Will you become one of these people? Will you allow the Good Shepherd to bring that wave of healing into your soul and through you to those around you?

Because here's the promise: Learn the unforced rhythms of grace, and you'll recover your life.

SOUL CARE REFLECTIONS

1. Consider a pressing situation or relationship in your life right now. What do you hope for as Scenario A? What do you fear as Scenario B? What would you settle for as Scenario C? What are some steps you need to take to posture yourself for Scenario Q?

2. What physical object could you place in your home or office as a visual reminder of the reality of the unseen world? Or of God's goodness toward you day to day?

3. Describe an experience in which you were able to hold the hard and the good together.

4. What do you feel in your body right now as it relates to peace? Do you notice any tension? Shoulders, forehead, neck? Headache, fatigue, something else?

5. What kind of peace do you think the world gives? How have you experienced it? How is it different from the peace that Jesus gives?

6. What circumstances do you currently feel closed in by? Are there interior challenges you simply cannot untangle? Financial constraints that you simply cannot overcome? Relational misses that are too far gone to repair? What would it mean to you for Jesus to show up and speak peace to your soul in this situation?

7. As you live and lead from a healthy soul, what contexts and relationships might experience the potential for healing?

Acknowledgments

So many people's hands, hearts, and minds have made this book possible.

Scott Beck, Wess Stafford, Jason Malec, Albert Tate, and Angie Ward challenged me to write a book that would get the message of Soul Care out into the world. Your voices and strategic introductions helped me reengage with writing after many years. Thank you.

Shawn Smucker brought much-needed leadership, wisdom, business savvy, industry knowledge, and skillful precision with words to this and other projects. A true Swiss Army knife collaboration partner! He and Maile and their family have become my friends. He makes the pressing of ideas into words look effortless, but it's work. Thank you.

With great kindness, patience, and expertise, Andrew Wolgemuth endured sifting through my many ideas until we found that one that we hoped would resonate. He then skillfully shepherded that idea through to an amazing partnership with NavPress and Tyndale. May this be just the beginning. Thank you.

Dave Zimmerman and Caitlyn Carlson and the teams at NavPress and Tyndale have brought not only the expertise of publishing but also a deep personal commitment to this message. We have been on this journey together. The manuscript was greatly enhanced not only by typical editorial improvements but also by a deep understanding of the nuance, context, and obstacles involved in facing these topics. What you read here is far better because of Caitlyn's dedicated and skillful shaping. Thank you.

The design team at Tyndale crushed the cover design. Thank you.

Zane and Jean Blackmer uniquely enabled the vision for Whisper Ranch to come to life. And they navigated the devastation of the Marshall Fire and the challenges of rebuilding alongside us. As couples, ours has been a journey of big dreams, bold prayers, facing fears, and the terrifying, life-giving invitation to hope. Hope for the future, hope for revival, hope for community and healthy leaders and stronger families. Thank you.

Jeff Caliguire, my college sweetheart and husband of many years, has evolved and grown with me since we met at Cornell in 1984. What an unexpected journey it has been! This has been a story of our ministry, our brokenness, our healing, and our transformation. Our beloved Whisper Ranch has been refined by fire. *We* have been refined by fire. We are better for it, and we are still in the game. The best is yet to come! Thank you.

Notes

CHAPTER 1 | A BURNED-OUT SOUL

1. Pastor, creative, and Bible scholar Tim Mackie first pushed me to realize the depth of biblical integration with these two words, *psychē* and *nephesh*.
2. Dallas Willard, *Renovation of the Heart: Putting on the Character of Christ*, 20th anniv. ed. (Colorado Springs: NavPress, 2021), 213.

CHAPTER 2 | RECOVER YOUR LIFE

1. Parker J. Palmer, *Let Your Life Speak: Listening for the Voice of Vocation* (New York: Jossey-Bass, 1999), 64.

CHAPTER 3 | THE GARDEN OF DESOLATION

1. "The Twelve Steps," Alcoholics Anonymous, accessed December 7, 2023, https://www.aa.org/the-twelve-steps.
2. Lewis B. Smedes, *The Art of Forgiving: When You Need to Forgive and Don't Know How* (New York: Ballantine Books, 1996), 171.

CHAPTER 4 | A PAGE, A PERSON, AND A PLAN

1. Harvard Health Publishing, "5 Surprising Benefits of Walking," December 7, 2023, https://www.health.harvard.edu/staying-healthy/5-surprising-benefits-of-walking.
2. Much of the material in Julian Sancton's book *Madhouse at the End of the Earth: The Belgica's Journey into the Dark Antarctic Night* (New York: Crown, 2021) comes from the journals of those on board the *Belgica*.
3. Allison Fallon, *The Power of Writing It Down: A Simple Habit to Unlock Your Brain and Reimagine Your Life* (Grand Rapids, MI: Zondervan, 2021), 101.

4. "Why Everyone Should Keep a Journal—7 Surprising Benefits," Kaiser Permanente, March 24, 2020, https://healthy.kaiserpermanente.org /southern-california/health-wellness/healtharticle.7-benefits-of-keeping-a -journal. See also K. Klein and A. Boals, "Expressive Writing Can Increase Working Memory Capacity," *Journal of Experimental Psychology*, September 2001, vol. 130, 520–533.

5. Robert Masters, "Spiritual Bypassing: Avoidance in Holy Drag," accessed December 7, 2023, https://www.robertmasters.com/2013/04/29/spiritual -bypassing.

6. This is my interpretation of Janet Hagberg's framework outlines in *Real Power: Stages of Personal Power in Organizations*, 3rd ed. (Salem, WI: Sheffield, 2002).

7. Jim Wilder and Michel Hendricks, *The Other Half of Church: Christian Community, Brain Science, and Overcoming Spiritual Stagnation* (Chicago: Moody Publishers, 2020), 91.

8. Warren S. Brown and Brad D. Strawn, *The Physical Nature of Christian Life: Neuroscience, Psychology, and the Church* (New York: Cambridge University Press, 2012), 87.

9. Mindy Caliguire, *Spiritual Friendship* (Westmont, IL: InterVarsity Press, 2007), 53–71.

10. Stephen A. Macchia, *Crafting a Rule of Life: An Invitation to the Well-Ordered Way* (Downers Grove, IL: IVP Books, 2012); Adele Ahlberg Calhoun, *Spiritual Disciplines Handbook: Practices That Transform Us*, rev. and expanded ed. (Downers Grove, IL: IVP Books, 2015); and John Mark Comer, *Rule of Life* (podcast).

CHAPTER 5 | BEYOND SURRENDER

1. Thomas R. Kelly, *A Testament of Devotion*, reprint ed. (New York: HarperOne, 1996), 124.

2. Julian of Norwich, *Showings*, trans. Edmund College and James Walsh (Mahwah, NJ: Paulist Press, 1978), 194.

3. Dallas Willard, *Renovation of the Heart: Putting on the Character of Christ* (Colorado Springs: NavPress, 2021), 152.

CHAPTER 6 | CULTIVATING HEALTHY SOUL SOIL

1. Thanks to Jim Wilder et al.'s *Joyful Journey: Listening to Immanuel* (Lexington, KY: Shepherd's House, Inc., 2015), I've learned so much about this and how important our capacity for joy is for us as humans.

2. Jim Wilder, "Joy Changes Everything," *Conversations* 12, no. 2 (Fall/Winter 2014): 47.
3. Wilder, "Joy Changes Everything."
4. Wilder, "Joy Changes Everything."
5. Wilder, "Joy Changes Everything."

CHAPTER 7 | SHY AND FEARLESS

1. Jim Collins, "Level 5 Leadership: The Triumph of Humility and Fierce Resolve," *Harvard Business Review*, January 1, 2001, https://hbr.org/2001/01/level-5-leadership-the-triumph-of-humility-and-fierce-resolve-2.
2. Richard Rohr, *Falling Upward: A Spirituality for the Two Halves of Life* (San Francisco: Jossey-Bass, 2011), 128.
3. Dallas Willard, *Hearing God: Developing a Conversational Relationship with God* (Downers Grove, IL: IVP, 2021), 52–53.
4. Scot McKnight, from personal conversations and comments made during his 2021 session at The Apprentice Gathering, recorded on YouTube, https://www.youtube.com/watch?v=GO-jv4zJVEY&ab_channel=ApprenticeInstituteatFriendsUniversity.
5. Andrew Murray, *Humility: The Journey Toward Holiness* (Bloomington, MN: Bethany House, 2001), 57.

CHAPTER 9 | THE HARDEST TASK

1. Heather Cherry, "The Benefits of Resting and How to Unplug in a Busy World," *Forbes*, January 15, 2021, https://www.forbes.com/sites/womensmedia/2021/01/15/the-benefits-of-resting-and-how-to-unplug-in-a-busy-world/?sh=47e615662133.
2. Cherry, "The Benefits of Resting."
3. Cherry, "The Benefits of Resting."
4. David Burkus, "Research Shows That Organizations Benefit When Employees Take Sabbaticals," *Harvard Business Review*, August 10, 2017, https://hbr.org/2017/08/research-shows-that-organizations-benefit-when-employees-take-sabbaticals.
5. I truly hope you will consider doing the same and helping each other on this path. Maybe start a Sabbath group with friends and text each week to let each other know when that imaginary line has been crossed. Or join our monthly semi-silent retreats online! You can find out more here: https://www.soulcare.com/collective.

CHAPTER 10 | SOUL FLOURISHING

1. The Twelve Steps," Alcoholics Anonymous, accessed December 7, 2023, https://www.aa.org/the-twelve-steps.

2. Cornelius Plantinga, Jr., *Not the Way It's Supposed to Be: A Breviary of Sin* (Grand Rapids, MI: Eerdmans, 1996), 10.

NavPress is the book-publishing arm of The Navigators.

Since 1933, The Navigators has helped people around the world bring hope and purpose to others in college campuses, local churches, workplaces, neighborhoods, and hard-to-reach places all over the world, face-to-face and person-by-person in an approach we call Life-to-Life® discipleship. We have committed together to know Christ, make Him known, and help others do the same.®

Would you like to join this adventure of discipleship and disciplemaking?

- Take a Digital Discipleship Journey at **navigators.org/disciplemaking**.
- Get more discipleship and disciplemaking content at **thedisciplemaker.org**.
- Find your next book, Bible, or discipleship resource at **navpress.com**.

 @NavPressPublishing

 @NavPress

 @navpressbooks